Oshkosh

Land Of
Lakeflies, Bubblers
and Squeaky Cheese

To Roy

Preserve & Embrace
Local History
—
Be Curious - Learn

By
Randy R. Domer

First published by Dog Ear Publishing
4011 Vincennes Rd
Indianapolis, IN 46268
www.dogearpublishing.net

ISBN: 978-1-4575-3854-4

This book is printed on acid-free paper.

Printed in the United States of America

Cover Photos - Usage Permission Granted by:
Lakefly: ©entomart
Bubbler: Randy Domer
Cheese: ©2014 Wisconsin Milk Marketing Board, Inc.

*Dedicated to my wife, Karen...for her love, support,
encouragement, inspiration*

A man in life
Should plant a tree
And write a book to strive
To dedicate; in memory
For his descendants his experience
As a criterion of his labor,
Docile, ethic, love and science
Reminiscent. —-

-Fred Jacob Gerstmeyer

TABLE OF CONTENTS

INTRODUCTION

W riting about the history and memories of my hometown at first seemed a bit daunting. As I quickly discovered, research-ing can and will take you in many different directions. You must stay the course and choose which direction to follow as the scope of stories, subjects, and people have limitless boundaries.

In my first book, *Yesterday In Oshkosh…My Hometown,* my stories were mostly reminiscent of the 1950s and 60s – the adolescent time in my life growing up around the city I call home. I was delighted and energized by people who approached me at book signings and events like the Oshkosh Saturday Farmers Market, to say how much they enjoyed the book and how it unearthed memories of things they had long forgotten. I became encouraged by some who reminded me I had "forgotten" to write about this or that.

It's that encouragement which motivates me to uncover more sto-ries of people and events that make Oshkosh what it is today. This time I decided there would be no timeline boundaries and I would venture out to the rural areas surrounding our great city.

During my research, I discovered things previously unknown to me. It is my intent to delight the reader with new information and per-haps a few surprises along the way.

As the title of this book implies, I will cover many topics…some a bit out of the ordinary. A few of the questions I will answer include… *Why do we call a drinking fountain a Bubbler?…* and… *Where did those pesky lakeflies come from?… Were they always here?*

I'll take you on a journey back to a time when people's livelihood was made catching frogs. And I'll tell you about a local family whose tradition goes back more than a hundred years as cheese makers.

My research and travels have introduced me to some very interesting people. I'll write about some whose roots began in Oshkosh, but made their marks elsewhere. Other stories will include some who grew up here and never left, achieving personal success within the community in which they lived.

Through personal interviews, I will share a treasure trove of stories and experiences. Sit with me as I chat with Theda Eckstein, the daughter of Leonard Larson and learn of their family's deep tradition in early aviation history. Or listen to the late Warren Hergert as he describes how his family started in the dairy business and ended up selling sporting goods.

What makes many of these personal experiences and memories so special is they do not appear in any history book at the library. They cannot be found in the vaults of our local museum or the archives of the historical society. They exist only in the memories of those who lived them. If we do not capture and record them today, tomorrow they will be lost to the ages.

Join me now, as we visit historic Oshkosh in another place in time.

THE ORPHANAGE

In the 1950s, the west side of Oshkosh was considered the edge of town. Some folks called it wilderness country. Oshkosh Avenue, once known as West Algoma, and Sawyer Street were the main streets on the west side back then. We considered Witzel Ave, or Fourth Street Road, the southern edge of our domain. The land west of Sawyer to US Highway 41 and between Oshkosh Ave and Witzel was largely undeveloped land. Only a few homes, mostly farm houses, could be found and they were few and far between. No high school, no Pollock Pool, and no Garbage Hill.

Because our side of town was virtually undeveloped, we knew every nook and cranny, creek and woodland, and just about every resident's last name. A blue Schwinn was my main form of transportation and it served me well. It never left the above described boundaries of the west side, but covered every inch of it. That trusty set of wheels took me to the Tesch farm on Witzel Ave to play a game of baseball with the Tesch boys when they were between chores, over to Hergert's Sport Center on the north end of Sawyer Street, and occasionally we would even venture to Oshkosh Ave. That's where the Mueller Potter drugstore sold all of my favorite comic books and Mary's Toy and Tog's sold the model birds I loved to assemble and paint. Further down the road was the municipal golf course and across Highway 41 we liked to visit the Par 3 golf course and driving range located adjacent to the Hollow Log, a favorite Oshkosh bar and hot spot.

Oshkosh Ave was also where the EB Davis Children's Home was located. Known by most of us as "the Orphanage", the large, stately, beautiful home sat near what today is the corner of Oshkosh Ave and North Eagle Street. The orphanage was a place where unfortunate children would reside while being cared for or awaiting adoption. Sometimes children were placed in the home because a family situation deemed it necessary. As a child I remember our parents issuing empty threats when we misbehaved. "If you don't behave, I'm going to send you over to the orphanage to live!" Needless to say, parenting was a little different back then. Besides, we never believed they'd really do it. Each time I rode my bike past the orphanage, I would wonder what it was like to not have a home or parents. I recall some of the kids attending Roosevelt School and one day they would be there, then another day they would be gone. I didn't give it much thought then, but I assume it was because they'd been adopted and moved away.

Coles Bashford.

Photo Credit: Library of Congress Prints and Photographs Division. Brady-Handy Photograph Collection. Public Domain

The home we all knew as the Orphanage has rich history and wasn't always known as a home for orphans. The Greek Revival style home was built in 1855 on 65 acres of land as the residence of Coles Bashford, Wisconsin's first Republican governor. Bashford, known for his firm anti-slavery stance, was elected governor in 1856 and served only a single term.

That election year, however, was embroiled in controversy when the Democratic incumbent, William A. Barstow, claimed victory by a mere 157 votes, which caused Bashford to challenge that his opponent was fraudulent by forging election returns coming in from nonexistent precincts in the sparsely populated northern part of Wisconsin. So, on January 7, 1856 Bashford was quietly sworn in while not far away, on the same day, Barstow was publicly inaugurated with full ceremony. The Wisconsin State Attorney General filed quo warranty proceedings in the State Supreme Court to remove Barstow, who threatened he "would not give up his office alive." Soon after, failing in his attempt to challenge the State judicial system and feeling that public opinion had turned against him, Barstow resigned leaving the vacant office to his Lieutenant Governor, Arthur McArthur as acting governor. It was reported that

Bashford then rushed McArthur's office, along with the sheriff and a handful of followers in tow, with the court judgment in hand to claim his office. McArthur quickly left and Bashford remained to be recognized as governor.

But scandal continued to follow Coles Bashford. At the completion of his first term, Bashford declined renomination. Soon after, reports surfaced that Bashford and his staff had accepted bribes from the LaCrosse and Milwaukee Railroad Company in exchange for a major land grant. The allegations claimed that Bashford personally received $50,000 in stocks and $15,000 in cash while State Legislators and a Wisconsin State Supreme Court Justice received payoffs exceeding $400,000. It was said critical documents were destroyed by implicated politicians and Bashford allegedly cashed in his stock before the railroad closed its doors as a result of the investigation. He then fled the state, never to face prosecution.

In the 1870s, the house was remodeled into a Gothic Revival style home. Purchased by Oshkosh lumber baron Robert McMillen in 1875, the house underwent some significant changes. The main structure was two-stories high, had a three-quarter Georgian floor plan and a single story wing that extended to the north. The house had verge board under the eaves and featured high pitched gable roofs (which were raised) with hooded windows. Dormer windows in the attic were added as well. Also, a second story was added to the north wing as well as a rear addition. The McMillen family lived here until 1909.

In 1911, the property was purchased by the trust of recently deceased Elizabeth Batchelder Davis. Mrs. Davis formed an endowment in her will to fulfill her wish to house "orphaned girls under the age of 15 years and such other poor and neglected or destitute children." The home would be run by "honest, economical, and frugal persons…those who will be kind to the children and furnish them with plenty of plain, wholesome, well-cooked food." The reason for this, it is speculated, is that E.B. Davis wanted the people to be kind to the children and she didn't want the home to be poorly managed so the endowment would last a long time.

Little is known about Elizabeth B. Davis' early years, but we do know she was born in 1823 in the eastern part of the US. She married Joseph Davis from Uniontown, PA in the mid 1800s. It was believed that he became an orphan some years after he was born and lived in an orphanage most of his childhood years. As was quite common then, it

House as it appeared when occupied by McMillan in 1887.

Photo Credit Dan Radig

is also believed that Joseph was forced to work in the mills (a form of forced child labor) which may have given him the resolve to make it on his own. He worked in the construction trade allowing him to eventually start his own contracting business. He moved his business to Cincinnati in the 1840s and it was there he met and married Elizabeth.

In 1865, Joseph and Elizabeth moved to Oshkosh where the promise of growing his business was strong. Oshkosh was a new territory and its rapid growth created a robust demand for construction. Davis soon built a home at 91 Church Street where he lived with his wife and two sons. In 1868 he formed the Oshkosh Gas Plant, a coal gasification plant that generated coal gas to run the lights in the homes and in the city. In 1883, Davis sold the gas plant business to Oshkosh's prominent citizen, Edgar Sawyer. That business, as we know it today, is Wisconsin Public Service.

Joseph Davis passed away in 1888. Twenty two years later, Elizabeth died on November 11, 1910. Both of her sons had passed before her and she left in her will an endowment of $130,000 (which in today's economy would equal well over three million dollars). It is believed Elizabeth had an affinity for children and the premature loss of her own two sons may have been the reason for her generous and perpetual gift to the community.

So, per Mrs. Davis' wishes, the house was purchased for around $13,000 and opened as an Orphanage in May 1912. Located significantly west of the developed part of the city, the property was more like a farm than a house. The 65 acres included some buildings and livestock (chickens, cows, mules, and pigs) and an orchard of fruit trees. According to an *Oshkosh Daily Northwestern* article on June 6, 1914, it was reported "the Orphanage is supplied with fountain water".

Children filled the wagon under the scrutiny of the Matron, Mrs. Edwards and Superintendant Mr. Kimball. Circa 1912.
Photo Courtesy of Dr. Tim Ryan

The farm served two main purposes. It provided fresh food for the home and the chores provided excellent learning opportunities, teaching the orphans how to care for themselves. The *Northwestern* article continues to say:

At present, there are twenty-nine girls and boys, from one to fourteen years of age, living as a large family in moderate circumstances, with the matron as a mother. They are furnished with plenty of well-cooked wholesome food, our own milk and eggs, early and winter vegetables, butter, meats, also plenty of crackers and breakfast foods, pastry, fruits, and candy. Three regular meals with lunches [in] between. All are properly bathed and supplied with clean clothing each week and oftener if needed, the smaller children daily. The girls are taught housework, cooking and sewing, [and] some are taking instrumental and vocal music. All of school age attending public schools. Their standings and advancement give them great credit. We have good reason to be proud of their table manners, which in itself alone, proves their control and government. They are without exception kind and generous to one another. There is no quarreling. They love the matron, each calling her Nonnie.

Living in the Orphanage differed little from children raised at home or on a farm. Everyone was expected to lend a hand in those days and not only did the work help sustain the home, but taught valuable "life's lessons".

By the 1920s, the home became more of a group foster home as orphanages were vanishing due to the development of successful foster care programs. The home was administrated by a board of directors who selected individuals to provide for care of the children and property.

An *Oshkosh Daily Northwestern* article in 1930 writes about a visit from Santa sponsored by the Oshkosh Junior Chamber of Commerce. "*There are 29 youngsters at the home this year, and there will be packages for all. For some, there will be useful articles of clothing such as mittens, gloves, stockings or handkerchiefs. The younger boys and girls will get toys and games. All of them will receive candy, nuts, and fruit.*"

That same year, fears arose as some of the children exhibited signs of chicken pox and there was a possibility that the home might be quarantined for Christmas. It was later determined all the children were well in time for the holiday festivities.

The role of the home changed slightly in the 1960s as reported by *The Oshkosh Daily Northwestern* in their Feb. 6, 1965 edition. The article headline read **"Children's Home Playing New Role"**. The article stated *"Elizabeth Batchelder Davis Children's Home...began another new role in the care of youngsters Friday with an announcement by the corporation of arrangements for use of the facility as a group home for teenage boys."* The home at this time was being managed by Mr. and Mrs. Richard E. Engle as foster parents. The new arrangement authorized group care for a maximum eight boys, ages 13-19 years old. The children would live in the home until the age of 19 or 20, if still in school. The article continued *"[County welfare director Norman] Whitford and acting board chairman Robert R. Thompson joined in expressing satisfaction that once again the E. B. Davis Home will adjust to the changing concepts and continue to shelter neglected, dependent or delinquent children at the same time preserving its identity."* The placement of individuals into the home was made by the welfare department based on individual needs. The county welfare department also provided casework services including supervision of each boy and counseling with the foster parents.

The house became a State Historic Landmark in 1976 and was dedicated by the Winnebago County Historical and Archaeological Society with a marker that same year as part of the national bi-centennial celebration.

In 1990, the house became the Davis Child Care Center and was used accordingly until a new structure was erected in 2004. One year later, the E.B. Davis Foundation announced plans to demolish the historic house. Despite the efforts of a local group of individuals formed specifically to save the house and in spite of a fund raising effort and the house being placed on the Wisconsin Trust's "10 Most Endangered" list, the battle to save the house was lost.

On May 4, 2006, the house was razed. Heavy equipment moved in and brought the historic old home to the ground. Gone was the home of Wisconsin's first Republican governor. Gone are walls that held the memories of young children struggling to find their way while growing up to fit into society and live normal, productive, and happy lives.

I am pleased to say that today the dream of Elizabeth Batchelder Davis still lives. This inspiring story, that started over 100 years ago, today still serves the needs of children in the Oshkosh area. The E.B. Davis Children's Center, now located adjacent to the site of the original historic house, is still faithful to the wishes of Elizabeth B. Davis by offering programs that provide emotional growth and well being in the development of children. Children learn through programs that educate and help develop social, ethical, and emotional skills in a safe nurturing environment designed to help them reach their fullest potential. The Center cares for children 11 years old and younger and is accredited by the National Association for the Education of Young Children.

Sources: Milwaukee Journal Sentinel, December 10, 1998; *Oshkosh Daily Northwestern* June 6, 1914, Dec.24, 1930 and Feb. 6,1965; bioguide.congress. gov/scripts/biodisplay.pl?index=B000219; E.B. Davis Child Care Center; Oshkosh-One Hundred Years A City, 1853-1953, Clinton F. Karstaedt, Editor; wipreservation.org/blog/tag/coles-bashford-house/; Oshkosh Public Museum Past Perfect Photo Collection

LAKEFLIES

E ach spring, local residents gather along the lakeshore to shake off the doldrums of cabin fever, bid farewell to old man winter, and welcome the rejuvenation of spring. The drab dredges of winter are now replaced with lush green grass, bursting tree buds, and flowers emerging from their long winter nap bringing a much needed splash of color along with the promise of new life. People are raking lawns while Mother's Day invites families to come together. Fragrant lilac bushes are in full bloom and fishermen are enjoying the annual return of walleyes and white bass from their upstream spawning grounds back into the surrounding lakes.

It is one of the most wonderful times of the year. But it is more than fish and flowers that make their annual grand entrance here.

Communities located along the Lake Winnebago shoreline are treated each season to the return of midges (Chironomus plumosus) or better known by locals as...the lakefly.

This event, I will go as far as calling it a phenomenon, occurs each spring when ideal water temperatures initiate the arrival of the dreaded lakefly that has lain dormant on Lake Winnebago's murky bottom since last season. The emergence is a sight to behold. When the "hatch" is in full force, swarms of these pesky little flies will attach themselves to anything and everything within a short distance of the waters edge. The number of flies in any one area is always relative to the wind. Not strong flyers by nature, the lakeflies will go where the winds blow them, and usually in big numbers. We have found that on days with an off shore wind, the number of lakeflies is fairly low. But on days with a southerly or easterly wind, it can be described as "plague-like".

Usually more of a nuisance than anything, they don't bite or sting but actually act like little kamikaze pilots, flying into to your eyes, ears, nose, and mouth. Each season I usually consume my share of lakeflies while mowing the lawn. If you fail to keep your mouth closed, you are assured of having at least one of them dive bomb in and catch in the back of your throat, provoking what I like to call the "lakefly yak"...that is the sound you make trying to get that little bugger up out of your throat, usually to no avail. And swatting them only serves to leave a dark green stain on your clothing that can be difficult to remove.

Stories about lakeflies from our elders rank right up there with "walking three miles to school, through four feet of snow, uphill in both directions". One old timer liked to tell me, "The flies were so heavy one year we had to scrape them off the sidewalk with snow shovels!"

It's also a commonly known fact that the flies thrive and reproduce in Lake Winnebago, but are quite rarely found in the upland waters of Lake Butte des Morts and Lake Poygan. I turned to a friend of mine to find out why. Richard P. Mason lives in Neenah and has dedicated much of his life to archaeology. He and his late wife, Carol Mason, are both locally noted and recognized archaeologists and did much of their field research in Winnebago County and the surrounding areas.

In April of 1993, Mason, along with members of the Robert Ritzenthaler Chapter of the Wisconsin Archeology (sic) Society, published a report titled *Archaeology, Cavalry, and Lakeflies*. Mason and his fellow colleagues wondered if early settlers and Native Americans had to deal with the ugly swarms of these pesky flies. Why would they decide to build villages along the shoreline among the flies when it would have been more comfortable a bit further inland? Is it possible that lakeflies were not present then?

These questions were nagging at Mason, who decided it was time to investigate further. In his research, he found reports indicating the presence of lakeflies in Lake Winnebago back to the early 1900s. They were first reported by A.C. Burril, a cavalryman from Troop A of the Wisconsin National Guard who camped with his unit just south of Neenah Wisconsin. Burril encountered swarms of lakeflies while riding on horseback near the Neenah rifle range. His report detailed the obnoxiousness of being among midge habits at swarming time. He also noted the whole line of horses would be sneezing and coughing incessantly at times.

So how did it all begin, you ask?

Local residents recorded swarms of flies as early as 1908, when algae covered Lake Winnebago with a thick, green coating that spanned many square miles. The algae bloom on the lake increased due to several factors.

First, the construction of the dams at Neenah and Menasha in the 1850s raised the waters of Lake Winnebago approximately a meter, causing it to become static. Large, static bodies of water have a tendency to become eutrophic if the nutrient load increases. [Author's Note: Eutrophic by definition is a body of water rich in nutrients supporting a dense plant population; the decomposition of which kills animal life by depriving it of oxygen.]

Shortly after the dams were built, upstream logging activities along the Wolf River denuded much of Wisconsin's virgin white pine forest. The Wolf River was used to transport logs downstream to Lake Poygan and onto Oshkosh where 24 sawmills were in operation. With the tree cover and root system gone, the cutover lands were beginning to erode into the river and millions of tons of fertile top soil were carried down the Wolf along with forest litter, duff (partially decomposed leaves and needles), and logs. The soil, litter, and duff eventually deposited into Lake Winnebago, along with the sawdust and bark from the sawmills. In 1874, it is reported 205 million board feet of lumber were sawn in Oshkosh and rafts of sawdust, sometimes miles long, could be observed floating on the big lake. The load-carrying capacity of the Wolf River was greatly reduced upon reaching the large static waters of Lake Winnebago, resulting in a thick blanket of sludge accumulating on the bottom of the lake. Previously, an 8 inch layer of white marl covered the lake bottom. White marl is a naturally occurring, fine, crumbly mixture of clay and limestone, often containing shell fragments and other minerals. It is believed the white marl formed over a period of about 8,000 years.

As the human population of Oshkosh increased, the waters of Lake Winnebago became more turbid as the seston, or organic particulate matter found in water, increased the nutrient load. Much of the cutover land upstream was now being plowed into farmland and the increased runoff caused water levels to fluctuate drastically. The widespread destruction of wetlands, due to poor drainage practices and the introduction of carp, added even more seston and turbidity. By 1924, Lake Winnebago was also suffering from severe sewage pollution from Oshkosh and Fond du Lac.

All of the conditions needed to support a nuisance population of lakeflies were now in place. The resulting black ooze on the lake bed provided a home for the larvae, the algae blooms provided food and the dwindling population of other insect species left a niche to be filled by lakeflies.

To further explain the sustainability of the lakefly population, the USDA Soil Conservation Service established the following water quality indicator guide:

> *As waters become increasingly eutrophied, the abundance and species composition of bottom organisms change. Waters receiving few, if any, excess nutrients from agricultural or other sources are characterized by a high diversity of bottom dwelling organisms. Generally, in these very pristine waters, the diversity is high, but the number of each type is low. Generally, as nutrient quantities increase, populations of intolerant species recede. They are replaced by expanding populations of nutrient-tolerant species, such as chironomids. The usual pattern is that as nutrients increase over time, the number of species (species diversity or richness) decreases, while the population growth of a few species increases.*

The nuisance of lakeflies is not exclusive to Lake Winnebago. Many large, shallow, polluted lakes with sludge bottoms have them. Other lakes in Wisconsin, like Lake Pepin, have occurrences similar to Lake Winnebago.

The life of a lakefly is brief. Once the pupa makes its way to the surface of the water and emerges as a lakefly, its life span is a mere 3 to 11 days, depending on temperature and humidity. Cool weather typically prolongs their life. Just before the female dies, 1000 to 2000 eggs are laid on the surface of the water. The egg mass then settles to the bottom where it swells to several times its original size. In 3 to 14 days, the eggs hatch and become the redworm, or bloodworm, larvae. The larvae go through four stages of metamorphosis and filter feed on seston, decayed algae, and diatoms. They spend this stage of their life in "U" shaped tubes in the muddy bottom, where they are eagerly devoured by Lake Sturgeon and other bottom feeding fishes in the Lake Winnebago system. Many of the larvae fail to pupate before summer is over and are left to overwinter in the ice covered lake. In spring, usually the last two weeks of May when the water temperature reaches 50 degrees Fahrenheit, the pupae move to the surface. Upon reaching the surface, the pupae emerge from their skins and take flight within 15-30 seconds. The fly immediately heads toward shore at a speed of 8 mph plus the speed of the wind.

Swarming occurs throughout the daylight hours and, although most prevalent at dawn and dusk. The swarms are primarily made up of males, as females will enter the swarm only to mate. Swarms will often form over trees and roads, as the slow flying midge seeks warmth.

Some years, it seems the number of flies is greater than other years. Researchers explain the number of lakeflies is directly related to the nutrient level in the spring runoff. The larvae require diatom blooms to provide the feeding stimulus necessary for pupae development. In 1992, the spring runoff was minimal in the lower Wolf River due to the lack of snow cover. Most of the water in Lake Winnebago was derived from northern Wisconsin, which also did not have substantial snow cover and the water contained fewer nutrients due to less farming activity in the north. The lakefly hatch that season was delayed until August. A similar occurrence also took place in the winter of 1957-58.

River currents flowing downstream into Lake Winnebago keep the lakefly breeding ground precisely in Lake Winnebago, much to the delight of property owners living along the upstream lakes, rivers, and streams.

The life cycle of the lakefly has become an important part of the Lake Winnebago food chain and will remain so as long as the eutrophic conditions in the big lake remain unchanged.

Perhaps the nuisance of the lakefly should serve as both a reminder and a lesson of what happens when we alter the environment.

Sources: Fox Valley Archeology, Number 21, April 1992, *Archeology, Cavalry and Lakeflies*; Terrell, Charles R. and Patricia Bytnar Perfetti, 1989, *Water Quality Indicators Guide: Surface Waters*, U.S. Department of Agriculture, Soil Conservation Service, Washington D.C.

THE RADDATZ SUBMARINE

Over the years, history tells us of the many attempts to build a water vessel capable of submerging and resurfacing at will. Such crafts, often times built with "military needs" in mind, have been designed throughout the world all the way back to the 16th century. Some historians report the very first idea of a submarine came as early as 1580 when Englishman William Bourne offered a description he created for "a boat that could go underwater unto the bottom and come up again at your pleasure."

Dutch inventor Cornelius Drebbel is given credit for creating the first submarine. He operated his machine below the waters of the English Thames River at depths of twelve to fifteen feet between the years 1620-1624. According to accounts, Drebbel's invention was a "decked-over rowboat propelled by twelve oarsmen." Best described, "The boat was designed to have almost neutral buoyancy, floating just awash, with a downward sloping foredeck to act as a sort of diving plane. The boat would be driven under the surface by forward momentum...just as are most modern submarines. When the rowers stopped rowing, the boat would slowly rise."

Through the years, various concepts were tested like "pointy-ended vessels designed to be semi-submerged allowing it to sneak up and punch holes in enemy ships." Other ancient designs included filling goat-skin bags with water to sink, then squeezing the water out again to rise. [1]

Many designs were developed and tested over the years in an attempt to perfect the process to balance the science of weight versus displacement and create a nautical vessel that was fully functional and dependable.

The year was 1897, only one year before the Spanish American War. Oshkosh resident Richard Raddatz, a 26 year old graduate of the

Oshkosh Normal School, designed, invented, and built what was hailed at the time as the "World's First Navigable Submarine."

"Accounts describe him [Richard Raddatz] as a tall, spare young man. His appearance and bearing betokening that he has some object in life other than keeping himself well groomed."[3] Some say Raddatz's motivation began at the young age of 11 when he heard about the French government offering a million dollars to anyone building a successful submarine. Other speculation hints he may have been inspired by the Jules Verne novel *20,000 Leagues Under the Sea* written 27 years earlier.[3]

As intriguing as Jules Verne's undersea adventures were to an aspiring young entrepreneur, it was all just fantasy. Sub nautical navigation had not yet been functionally developed and it would be another three years before the US Navy would even have their first submarine.

As he began work to fulfill his dream, Raddatz was reticent and secretive about his project. Much of the work was performed in a barn or behind an eight foot fence. To build his vessel, Raddatz incorporated the assistance of August C. Schulz, a local cooper and lumber company operator. Schulz was a first generation German who founded the Oshkosh Cistern and Keg Company (1891), later known as the Oshkosh Tank and Lumber Company. The business was originally located in Oshkosh at 213 Sixth Street, later to be relocated to 428 Seventh Street around 1897. Schulz was a manufacturer of beer and wine barrels, brewery vats, cisterns and tanks. [3]

Schulz's granddaughter, Charlotte Schulz Christen, says she was told by her father, Henry, that August sold barrels to bootleggers during Prohibition, a practice that caused him to be censured from the pulpit of his church by the parish priest. The family says that he stopped going to church after this happened and instead spent his Sunday mornings taking his dog for a walk and working in his shop. Son Henry Schulz told family members how he and his brother Herbert drove out in the country to deliver barrels, often down long, dark, winding roads. It was explained that bootleggers needed a lot of barrels because they burned them after each use to destroy potential evidence of their wrongdoing. Charlotte told me a story that her father shared with her a few years before his death. "My father, Henry, and his brother Herbert were on a delivery trip one day when they noticed a six-toed cat near a barn. Figuring their mother would like the cat, they swooped it up and took

August Schulz, seen here standing beside his wife Mary, was a cooper and a lumber company operator. He helped Raddatz design and build the submarine.

Photo credit: Charlotte Schulz Christen

it home to her." Charlotte mused on what the mother actually thought of this whole event and imagined she had a few choice words for her sons. She also wondered how they got close enough to notice the cat had six toes!

Raddatz's first design proved unsuccessful as the original prototype built in 1894 included a hull designed by August Schulz that was built from wood. The problem with the design was it didn't sink...it floated instead. That drove the young inventor back to the drawing board where he began to create a model fabricated from metal. The cigar-shaped, hollow metal cylinder resembled more than anything else, a locomotive boiler, except it was pointed on both ends.[3]

The new vessel measured sixty-five feet in length and over four feet in diameter on the inside. Beginning sixteen feet from each end the submarine tapered sharply to a point, the thought being that a submarine could be used for ramming ships in wartime. Two conning towers eighteen inches in diameter projected above the water and at the rear a propeller. Below the propeller were rudders used for steering the craft. The estimated weight of the vessel was 35 tons.

During construction, lack of adequate funding caused Raddatz to look to the Oshkosh community for support. Support and financial assistance for his project came from a small group of Oshkosh residents which included William and Otto Konrad who backed the inventor "...to the extent of $3,000".[2] The 1895 Bunn's Winnebago County Directory lists William Konrad's occupation as *"Furniture and undertaking. Upholstering and picture framing. A large and fine line of furniture. Doing business at 33 Main Street in Oshkosh"*. The venture began in a barn owned by the Konrads. William's son Charles, then 16 years of age, became Raddatz's eager and willing helper.[2]   Charles became close with Raddatz and accompanied him each step of the way.

Oshkosh resident, and Konrad descendant, Gary Konrad remembers his grandfather George Konrad describing what he remembered as a child. "My grandfather claimed construction of the sub occurred in the rafters of the Konrad barn which was located on what we know today as Bay Shore Drive, where the former DNR building now stands. At one point when they were ready, they built skids out of beams and slid the sub down to the river's edge." The sub was kept out of sight in a boat house there, where preliminary water testing was done. An eight-foot wooden fence was also erected to protect the privacy of the project while in dry-dock.

On June 26, 1897, Raddatz's submarine was ready for its first test launch. The launch was scheduled to take place in the Fox River. Before the launch, scores of people and even newspaper reporters who "caught wind" of the proposed launch, gathered along the river banks in curiosity. Raddatz told a reporter "This is only an experiment. Successful, I hope, and I do not want to talk too much about it at this stake." Besieged by the press for mechanical explanations, Raddatz said, "By her machinery she can be sunk to any depth and maintained at any depth either in motion or at rest. She is supplied with air and in case of an accident be returned to the surface immediately. One man can operate her by means of levers and buttons in the cabin. A dozen men could be crowded into her." [2]

The operating system of the newfangled vessel was described in an article published by Oshkosh's *The Paper* on December 19, 1968. "Downward movement…was attained by taking in water into two hot water tanks of the variety that are used for bathroom purposes. The vessel was brought to the surface by forcing water out of her tanks by means of a large bicycle foot pump." Not really state of the art technology, but certainly functional.

Details of the launch are recorded in a report written in 1933 by Charles "CC" Konrad, who accompanied Raddatz on the maiden voyage. Konrad writes, "Try, if you can, to visualize yourself in a country where automobiles are unknown, airplanes a dream and surface boats are still slow and unwieldy. Such was the situation in 1897. And with that background in mind, can you not feel the excitement that was

One of the few photos known to exist of the Raddatz submarine. Although he never patented the design, Raddatz was very secretive about his project, hiding his work in a barn, a boathouse, or behind an eight foot fence. Circa 1897.

Photo Courtesy of Ed Tiedje

caused by our daring experiment to penetrate a region still unexplored." Konrad acknowledges the privilege and good fortune to be closely associated with Richard Raddatz and to accompany him on many trips beneath the water.

On the day of the launch, Konrad recalls, "A number of people had discovered when the boat was to be launched and this group congregated at the river bank as preparations were made for a test. Everyone watched wonderingly, and with a tremor of excitement, the long black, low lying craft floating in the river current. This mysterious looking vessel, one of the world's first practical submarines, was a strange sight in those days, especially in an inland city."

Konrad went on to describe the feeling as he and Raddatz boarded the submarine. As he scanned the crowd he could see the excitement and anxiety in their eyes. "...Mr. Raddatz and I climbed down into the dark depths of the boat through the funnel shaped conning tower. Just before closing the cover on the tower the inventor called to the assembled group, 'We are going to submerge and lie on the river bottom for fifteen minutes.'"

Edward F. Kennedy, reporter for *The New York World* accompanied Raddatz and Konrad on the historic launch. His account of the epic event was published in *The Daily Northwestern* on July 3, 1887 in a story titled "Jules Verne in Oshkosh":

> *The crowd watched as the boat submerged as predicted. Observers held their breath with anticipation and fear. As minutes passed, not even a ripple was seen on the water. After ten minutes the crowd began to grow restless. At the fifteen minute mark, there was no sign of the submarine surfacing as Raddatz had indicated earlier. Anxiety turned into deep concern. After twenty-five minutes the crowd was certain disaster had struck. Some shouted, 'Call the fire department!' while others were ready to organize a dredging operation.*
>
> *Suddenly, the large black snout, like that of a huge alligator, broke the water surface. In a moment the conning towers appeared, and soon after the sub was sitting safely dockside. The lid on the conning tower opened and the men emerged, apparently none the worse for their experience. Cheers, elation and shouts of relief came from the crowd. The first trial was deemed a success.*

Passenger/reporter Edward Kennedy described the experience from his perspective. "The descent was really a voyage. The boat traversed a distance of half a mile and remained stationary several minutes in the draw of the Chicago and Northwestern railroad bridge. This was done to test its machinery, as the current is very swift, and Mr. Raddatz desired to prove that the boat could be held stationary in a rapid current…While thus anchored a river steamer passed through the draw. She could be seen distinctly." Kennedy revealed his anxiety as he boarded the boat. "I must confess that it was not without misgivings that I stepped within what looked like a floating coffin, and the sensations of that voyage I will never forget. After the party became seated the manhead was closed down and secured, shutting out all sounds from outside except a vague murmur which it was hard to believe, was all that could be heard of the shouts of the spectators on the bank. Immediately on discovering that I was hermetically sealed within the iron vessel the fear arose that the air supply being completely shut off there would be difficulty in breathing, if not actual suffocation…".

Modifications by the inventor continued to improve the functionality of the submarine. A contraption was designed using the gears from a bicycle to which they attached the shafting and propeller. The propeller was put into motion by the same action one uses to ride a bicycle.

Over the coming months, Konrad and Raddatz performed many underwater trips and had some interesting stories to share. Konrad writes,

> *While navigating near the bottom of the river we rammed one of the piers of the Northwestern railway bridge. These piers were constructed in a manner with various piles being driven in the bottom of the river forming a cluster and separating at the bottom something like a foot or more from each other. Into these we had become wedged tightly. We tried to come up but the gauge would not show any rise and we knew we were stuck fast. Our pointed end had certainly demonstrated its ability to ram whatever got in its way, but with results entirely unexpected and overlooked by the inventor. Surely the ramming of a ship would have entailed greater consequences. I made the remark to our inventor, Mr. Raddatz, 'How are we going to get back to the surface?' He made a peculiar remark, even to himself, when he stretched out his arm and rested his chin on his hand, and said, 'What a piece of paper might have been but isn't.' This was so ridiculous sounding to me that I laughed out right at him but exclaimed 'Dick, this is no time for idle talk, we have to get out of this because the air is getting heavy.' He asked 'What should we do Charlie?' I replied, 'Do what I tell you and when I say **RIGHT** I will propel forward and you turn the rudder left and when I say **LEFT** I will propel backward and you turn the rudder to the right and in that way we will wiggle ourselves out.*

After a few attempts, Konrads' plan succeeded and the sub worked itself free of the pilings.

Another mishap occurred as Raddatz himself described in a *Milwaukee Sentinel* article (date unknown) kept in the Oshkosh Public Museum files. "I had one experience with my first boat that I shall never forget. It was provided with large windows, filled in with heavy plate glass. One day in navigating the bottom of the Fox River, the boat ran into some piling and broke in one of the windows. The water rolled in upon us by the barrel full, but I managed to pull the lever and we shot up to the surface so quickly the boat almost jumped out of the water. Fortunately the broken window was above the water line when we were on the surface."

During their underwater voyages, Raddatz would marvel at seeing fish in their natural environment and the vegetation that thrived on the river bottom. The August 14, 1898 edition of *The Sunday Chronicle*, a Chicago newspaper, reported on one such occasion. Raddatz agreed to take a reporter along for the ride, this time on Lake Michigan. The apprehensive reporter reluctantly agreed and climbed into the iron tube. The sub was cruising just five feet below the surface when Raddatz urged the reporter to look through the tiny peepholes designed to see outside the vessel. Schools of perch and herring were attracted by the appearance of the strange visitor. Small minnows, curious and inquisitive, came up to the small holes to investigate. Suddenly Raddatz exclaimed "Holy smoke!" The anxious reporter cried out "What's the matter??!!" as he bumped his head against the top of the iron boat. Raddatz explained "Say, you should've seen that fish! 'Twas bigger than a whale!"

By the end of the season, more money was needed to keep the project going. Raddatz needed to continue improvements and had dreams of building another submarine. The Konrads could no longer agree to finance him, so the submarine was sold to a Milwaukee resident named Mr. Lyendecker, who continued to experiment with the inventor. In the coming years, Raddatz would relocate from Oshkosh to Milwaukee where he would build two more submarines. He never patented his original design as he felt there was more value in selling the "secrets" of his design along with the submarine to potential buyers like a foreign government.

The work eventually expanded to Philadelphia where experiments were done with the famous John P. Holland who launched a successful submarine about a year later.

Newspaper articles reporting the final resting place for the Raddatz submarine vary, but all agree it was near Milwaukee on Jones Island where the iron-clad boat was put into dry-dock. Some reports conjectured that it is there where the sub was abandoned and eventually rusted away, while others claim it was cut up and sold as scrap metal. Efforts to locate the boat in recent years have been unsuccessful.

According to his own records, Raddatz claimed to have made over three-hundred trips with his invention. Blueprints of the Raddatz Submarine can be found today, nestled in the archives of the Oshkosh Public Museum.

In 1898, Richard Raddatz married his wife, Anna, in Milwaukee where he worked for E.P. Ellis and Allis Chalmers until around 1921. Together they had two children, Ronald and Anna.

Inventor Richard Raddatz died in Milwaukee in 1933. Builder August C. Schultz died in his Oshkosh home in January of that same year.

Sources: (1) http://www.submarine-history.com/NOVAone.htm#1623; (2) Appleton Post Crescent, October 15, 1967; (3) *Oshkosh Daily Northwestern*, May 26-27, 1979; (4) CC Konrad Program to Winnebago County Arch. & Hist. Soc., Nov. 14,1933 on file Oshkosh Public Museum; (5) Boston Sunday Post 1898 article written by Louis V. DeFoe; (6) *Oshkosh Daily Northwestern*, April 14, 1898; (7) Oshkosh Public Library report written by Adam Kohler, Nov. 2014

HERGERT QUALITY DAIRY

S pring is the time of year when you become anxious to resume outdoor activities such as working in the yard, buying garden seeds - and fishing! Oshkosh is surrounded by wonderful lakes and rivers and is famous for its spring fishing. Early season fishing kicks off with the walleyes returning to the lakes of Winnebago, Butte des Morts and Poygan from its upstream waters after their annual spawning ritual. Once the walleyes have spawned and are back in their home lakes, the white bass follow, sometimes in huge numbers. It is without question the best time of year for fishermen.

It was a beautiful spring day in April 2012. Much of the nation was just emerging from one of the mildest winters on record. Minimal snowfall and record warm temperatures blanketed most of the central and eastern US. Here in Wisconsin we experienced much the same. "One of the warmest winters on record!" my neighbor exclaimed.

I decided it was time I became serious about fishing. I love to fish, but usually my efforts are confined to fishing off my dock or that of a friend. Each year I watch the boats gather on the numerous reefs which run from Garlic Island east and southeast toward Oshkosh. It is a famous spot for sportsmen, as the reefs provide good feeding areas and fish are usually found in good numbers in spring and most of the summer.

Well, I realized that if I was going to make a more dedicated effort of fishing, I needed to buy a fishing boat. So I stopped at Hergert Sport Center on Sawyer Street to check out their spring inventory. The business is owned by the Hergert family and has been for many years. I've known the Hergerts most of my life as my dad purchased a boat from them in the early 1960s and several of the Hergert kids were classmates of mine at Roosevelt and throughout high school. My dad knew the

Hergert brothers; Marvin, Warren and Bob. They were always behind the counter and the usual chit chat would begin as soon as we walked in the door. I always enjoyed accompanying my father to Hergert's because I liked listening to the back and forth banter. The store was always full of new boats and a large assortment of fishing baits and equipment. Dad would ask for a fishing report because he worked all week and wanted to know what the locals were catching, what baits they were using, and where they were catching them. The Hergerts always had the scoop and gladly shared those "closely guarded fishing secrets" which some of the local anglers held tightly to their vest.

I drove up alongside the store and parked my vehicle on Fillmore Avenue which runs along the south end of the store near the boat display area. I walked around to the main entrance on Sawyer St. and pulled open the door. It immediately struck me that things here hadn't changed much since the early days. The building's appearance looked the same as it did in the early 60s on the exterior. Then as I walked through the door, it felt the same too. A courtesy chime announced my arrival as I made my way toward the service counter, looking for Ralph Hergert. Ralph handles all the service end of the business and is not usually found behind the service counter, but I knew that's where I needed to start. Today the business is run by Bob Hergert, Warren's sons Ralph and Ron, and Mark Spanbauer, long time employee and friend of the Hergert family. Of the three, I knew Ralph best as we were close in age and went to Roosevelt school together, only a grade or two apart. Mark was on the phone but gave me the sign he would be with me in a minute.

I waited while Mark finished his call, then he greeted me with "Mr. Domer! What can we do for you today?" I, like many people, appreciate being recognized where they do business and always feel special when they are. I also prefer to support local merchants and family owned businesses as I appreciate the hard work that goes into owning and running a business successfully for so many years.

"I'm looking for Ralph," I responded. "I'm looking to buy a fishing boat." Mark paged Ralph, asking him of his whereabouts. "He's back in the boat storage shed," Mark informed me pointing toward the big metal building next door. I thanked Mark, then walked out the back door and spied Ralph as he was walking toward the retail store. Wiping some oil off his hands he spotted me. "Hey, what's up?" he asked. I told him and he said "Let's go inside."

As we walked back into the boat showroom, Ralph and Mark were talking with me about my boat needs and my name was mentioned in conversation. Suddenly, I heard a voice coming from behind the boats on display in the showroom. An elderly man stepped out and I immediately recognized the face and voice as Warren Hergert. "Did you say Domer?" Warren asked. Ralph introduced me to Warren, who had been sitting in a chair next to the window and well hidden behind the boat displays. I reached out and shook his hand saying "I'm not sure if you remember me." Warren looked up and said "Yeah, I remember you. Donny Domer. Donny is your dad, right? Sure, I remember." I assured him he was correct and we reminisced briefly about my dad and our visits to Hergert's Sports Center back in the 1960s. Ralph noted that his dad, Warren, comes in everyday around 9:30-10:00 am and sits by the window. "I enjoy it here," he said quietly. "I lost my wife not long ago, it was in 2011, and I come here because who wants to just sit around the house?" Warren continued on saying his wife's name was Elizabeth but everyone called her "Boots." "Back then, everyone hung around with people who lived nearby in the neighborhood. Boots lived across the street over there, and one day she came over and asked me to give her a ride on my motorcycle. From that time on we were together." He paused, looked around the room, and proceeded to tell me that he spent most of his life here in this building, and being there now helped occupy his thoughts. It was apparent he deeply loved and missed his wife.

I asked Warren about the family business and indicated that I knew it had originally started out as a dairy. "That's right," said Warren. "I used to make the ice cream, right here," he claimed as he pointed around the room.

We stood and made small talk for a few minutes, and then Warren looked at me and quietly said "I was diagnosed with colon cancer yesterday. I'm 83 years old and lost my wife recently." Saddened by this I replied, "Warren, I am so sorry to hear about your illness and the loss of your wife." Warren looked up at me, smiled and said, "That's all right Randy. It just means soon I'll be able to put my arms around my wife again." I didn't know what to say, but I was deeply moved by his soulful perspective on what was to come next in his life.

It was then I realized this would be a great story to write. I asked Warren if I could return another time to sit with him and learn about the family history in the dairy and sporting goods business. "Yeah, sure." he replied dryly. "Don't know if there's anything you'll find interesting or not, but go ahead." The years have not softened Warren Hergert. At 83 years old, he still believes in telling it like it is and pulling no punches. His language can be salty and spicy at times, but his face and expressions soften when he starts talking about the early years in business and of his family.

Unsure if I was going to write another book, I put this story on the back burner temporarily. But my conversation with Warren kept tugging at me. His comments on his wife touched me so. I strongly believe and feel that the experiences of people who have enjoyed long lives are held only within their precious memories. If not captured, those experiences will someday be lost to the ages.

It was almost a year later when I became inspired to write another book and I wanted to know more about the history of the Hergert family business. So, I stopped by to see if Warren was still willing to share his stories with me.

There he was, sitting in the same chair by the same south window, watching the traffic and passerbys. I couldn't help but wonder what his thoughts were as he gazed outside. I reminded him of our conversation and he uttered "Whatever." That was Warren's way of agreeing to meet with me again. We set a date and I promised to return with my tape recorder and tablet.

When I returned, Warren greeted me and led me to a place where we could sit and talk. He held out some papers and said, "Here, everything you want to know about us is in here." In his hand was an article from *The Oshkosh Northwestern* dated 2005 and featured the Hergert's 50-year celebration in business. Also included was an article of unknown origin that contained some of the business history of the family. I thanked Warren for the information and promised to return it once I had read it.

A short time later, I returned to sit with Warren. We then began to unravel the history of their family business. I asked him to take me back to when his family first started.

Without hesitation, Warren began, "My dad got into the dairy business in 1935. He was working at Paine Lumber as a draftsman, but he wasn't earning enough to sustain his family's needs. It was the depression era and my dad was too proud to accept 'relief'. So he went to a local farmer and bought a can of milk, which equaled about 40 quarts. He brought it home, bottled it up, took his Model A, and went from door to door until it was all sold. The next day he bought **two** cans of milk... and so on."

Philip and Anna Hergert worked side-by-side to build the dairy business which included enlisting the help of their children. "When we were old enough to do something, we pitched in." Warren said proudly. "Everyone in the family helped including us kids. We used to wash bottles in the basement by hand."

Philip Hergert started his new business in a small building erected in the yard of their home at 144 Sixth Ave. (now Van Buren Ave). Milk deliveries, which started at two o'clock in the morning, were made in the old family vehicle. This was necessary because there was no refrigeration at the time. "In the early days, milk was kept cold by using well water. Well water comes out of the ground at forty degrees and that's how the farmers kept milk cold until we could pick it up. At the dairy, we used ice boxes to keep the milk cold," Warren shared. He then continued, "When I was fourteen years old I had my own truck and my own route!"

Hergert Quality Dairy.
Photo Credit: Robert Hergert

Philip Hergert built a new building in 1948 to expand refrigeration capabilities. He added ice cream to expand their business model to offset sagging milk sales. Hergert Quality Dairy sold a complete line of dairy products in addition to milk and ice cream. Local favorites included cottage cheese, buttermilk, cream, chocolate milk, butter, and more.

"When we started there were 36 dairies in town. After pasteurization came, the farmers all started to quit." Most farms had their own version of a dairy then, but new laws on pasteurization forced most of them out of the dairy business. Refrigeration technology continued to improve during World War II and the onset of refrigeration started to move milk from home delivery to the supermarkets. "My brother Marv and I took over the business around 1948 when my dad had to quit due to health reasons. In 1952 my dad passed away," Warren informed me. Philip's wife Anna assumed the presidency of the company with Marv and Warren as vice presidents. At its peak, the dairy had 5 delivery trucks and eight employees. "Toward the end," Warren recalled, "it came down to just three dairies left in operation - Hergert, Sunlite and Guernsey Dairy. They were the three largest and lasted the longest." While Guernsey Dairy, or GDC as many of us remember it, was a dairy in the purest sense, Sunlite Dairy had two stores...one on North Main Street and another on Ohio Street, in the 800 block. Sunlite and Hergert both were renowned for delicious handmade ice cream. Each store had counters with stools for folks to sit and visit while enjoying a creamy delight.

Warren remembered when he made all the ice cream for the store. "I'd come in at 5 am and start delivering milk, and then I'd return to the store and make ice cream. Our ice cream was made from cream with 13% butter fat and what eventually took the business away from us was the supermarkets selling products with lower fat content product with only 8% butter fat. We also used real, natural bean vanilla where the larger companies used imitation vanilla. They made it cheaper so they could sell it for less."

Marv and Warren were keenly aware of the changes occurring around them and intuitively decided they needed to adjust strategies if they were going to remain successful in business. Customers could now buy milk at the grocery store for less than they could for home delivery. Warren explained that employee wages and the expense of maintaining delivery trucks became cost prohibitive.

"I did a lot of hunting and fishing while my brother Marv did a lot of boat racing," Warren said. "So we started the sporting goods business." In 1954, they built a small building next to the dairy to accommodate their new interest in sporting goods. Warren's son Ron added, "The new sport shop was named Westgate Sporting Goods." The new building was built along the south bank of Sawyer Creek across from where Pluswood operated a sawmill and manufactured plywood products. Previous to that, the site was part of the Paine Lumber Company which occupied that and much of the land where Rainbow Park is today. When the Hergerts decided to build on the site, they discovered about 4 inches of sawdust that had accumulated over the years. "We had sawdust from here all the way to the river," Warren stated. "When we built, we made sure the contractors dug down deep to the bedrock so we had good footings."

In 1956, Hergert's discontinued home milk delivery but still kept the ice cream store going until 1959 when they decided to exit the ice cream business and convert the space to expand their sporting goods offerings. The Westgate Sport Center, which began as a sideline to the dairy business, now required big changes. The Hergerts needed to transition their business from ice cream and milk to sporting goods. "Marv and I did the complete remodel. We had no money so we tore out the freezer and cooler ourselves. There wasn't anything my brother Marv couldn't build or fix," he added. Pointing to the north wall behind the service counter, he continued, "Those gun racks and wood cabinets over there, we built them." The original building where Westgate started is still standing today at the edge of Sawyer Creek and is used as a service and maintenance area.

In 1960, the youngest Hergert brother Bob graduated from college. The sporting goods business was growing and occupied larger space in what once was dedicated to dairy. Warren explained, "Bob had the choice to work someplace else or work with us and he decided to work with us...my brother Marv, me and my mother. It was the four of us."

The change in business from dairy to sporting goods however was not an easy transition. In those early years of establishing themselves as a sporting goods retailer, the Hergerts worked through some difficult times. "It reached a point where we made barely enough money to pay the bills," Warren told me. But through hard work and persistence, their effort came to fruition.

"By 1962, the County Clerk told me we were doing 25% of all hunting and fishing licenses in Winnebago County," Warren said proudly. But as time went on, the Hergerts saw their sporting goods business erode to the "big box" retailers. He also talked about other changes that impacted their business. "Boat storage was a big part of our business. Then people started building 3 car garages and we slowly watched that business slip away."

In 1980, Marvin Hergert died. Brothers Warren and Bob continued to run the business with the help of the next generation of Hergert kids quickly coming of age.

Warren says he quit working 21 years ago. "Originally I told them to take me off the payroll, but I'm not quitting. The first year I probably put in about 45 hours a week but that was less than I usually worked. Sixty hours back then was a short week! Our busy time was spring and fall and we'd put in 75-80 hours a week."

As we finished our conversation, Warren summarized, "If it wasn't for the service we provide, that means taking care of people, Hergert Sport Center wouldn't be here today."

I sat down with Bob on one of my return visits and enjoyed listening to the Hergert family business history from his perspective. Before college, Bob worked alongside his parents and brothers in the early dairy business. "As we said, it was truly a family business which meant everyone pitched in. At the age of twelve I helped with milk deliveries. There were two of us on the truck. One person drove while I ran milk up to the house and returned with empties. I learned how to pick up four bottles in each hand, which was always a little more difficult in winter when your fingers were freezing," Bob said with a smile. At age fourteen, Bob earned a temporary permit to drive which allowed him to operate the family delivery trucks. He also worked behind the ice cream counter and assisted with making ice cream, bottling milk, and washing and cleaning.

Bob remembers the early days in the dairy business very well. "When we started out at home bottling milk it was in the garage. We worked from that location until about 1940. Then my dad had the idea to buy a farm so he could have more control over his milk supply." He added, "He bought a farm out on Fourth Street Road just past Claireville Road and managed a small herd of dairy cattle. When the war ended he decided to move the business back in town to Sawyer Street. He sold the farm and used the money to expand the rapidly growing dairy business by adding ice cream and other quality dairy products. Also, my mother wasn't in favor of living so far out in the country so I'm sure that was part of the reason," Bob admitted with a knowing smile.

I asked Bob to help me visualize what the dairy and ice cream store would have looked like in the fifties. We walked through aisles of sporting goods as Bob pointed out where the ice cream counter once stood. "The counter was about 30' to 40' long and built by my dad. There were three ice cream dispensers, each measuring about 12' in length. Ice cream was made in five-gallon pails and we offered about twenty different flavors." He turned, waving his arm and said, "This is where the 'back bar' was located. It held the cash register, malt machine, ingredients for sundaes and the sort. At the south end of the counter was a big root beer barrel. We mixed and sold our own homemade root beer." He showed me where the original entrance doors, tables, and chairs were located and pointed to the far northwest corner of the room explaining there once stood a jukebox.

The Hergerts are very proud of their long standing affiliation with Mercury Marine. "We started with Kiekhaefer Mercury in 1957 and have been a Mercury dealer ever since," Bob informed me.

Today, Bob Hergert still works a full week and does everything including billing, waiting on customers, handling phones, and more. In my time spent with Bob, I noticed that he still has a youthful glow about him. I was amazed when he told me that he still snow skis, so I asked him if he would tell me his age. Bob looked at me with a twinkle in his eye, winked and said, "We really don't have to go there Randy, do we?"

Postscript: My interview with Warren Hergert began in 2012 and I made several trips back to see him into the late fall of 2013. I was deeply saddened to learn that Friday, March 21, 2014, Warren John Hergert passed away. In my talks with Warren, his love for his family and their closeness was evidenced by the Sunday morning breakfasts at his house with his family and his daily routine of coming to the store.

The loss of his beloved wife Boots affected him deeply. I could feel and hear it in his words when he spoke of her.

In my heart, I'd like to believe that today Warren has received his final wish. That is to put his arms around his beloved wife Boots once again.

ALASKA POPS

Mention the word "Popsicle®" and every kid's face will light up. We've all grown up eating Popsicles, but not like the ones we enjoyed in the 1950s.

A small Oshkosh company began doing business in the 1940s in a modest, little building on the corner of Spruce Street and Reed Avenue. Phil Nitkowski created a frozen treat and built a good business around a product named *Alaska Pop.*

The Alaska Pop was very much like the Popsicle brand we all have known and enjoyed for decades, only slightly different in shape. Popsicles were double frozen columns of fruit-flavored ice with two sticks protruding from the bottom. If one wanted to share, you simply broke it into two halves and each would have a stick of frozen fruity goodness to enjoy. Alaska Pops, however, were not intended for sharing. One solid block of fruit-flavored ice and one stick. The frozen treat was square-shaped; a bit wider at the bottom and slightly tapered toward the top. Carried in every grocery store in town, they were found in the frozen novelty section, wrapped in a paper sleeve with the Alaska Pop logo printed on the front.

Alaska Pops came in assorted flavors including cherry, orange, banana and even chocolate. My personal favorite was root beer!

Recently, I sat with Phil Nitkowski's daughter, Judy Engleman, and asked her to tell me about her family's historic business.

At first, Judy seemed a bit reticent. So many years has gone by and she didn't think she could remember much about the business. But once we started talking, details of her family business began to take shape.

"My father started the business in the mid 1940s" she said. "He conceived the idea because someone he knew had experienced some health issues and couldn't eat many kinds of foods. So he created and developed the Alaska Pop into something they could enjoy."

I asked Judy about something I had seen in the Oshkosh City Directory dated 1948. It listed her father as an "ice cream mfr". She clarified that for me "In the early years of business, dad created a product that was similar to what we know today as the Dreamsicle®." The item never really caught on and Nitkowski's attention turned to Alaska Pops.

The company name was originally listed as Frozen Products Co., and like most small family owned businesses, it was operated utilizing every member of the Nitkowski family. "My dad did everything. He worked on the production end and also ran deliveries to the local stores. My mom, Harriet, was the bookkeeper and my brother David and I worked various jobs on the production side. I was fourteen and my brother was one year older. Even my Grandmother, my dad's mom who lived near the store, worked alongside us" she said proudly. "Only a handful of other workers were employed, mostly friends and neighbors." Judy went on to explain from the perspective of a fourteen year old "On payday, each employee was given an envelope containing their salary. I believe they were paid in cash" she added.

As you would imagine, the frozen treat business is quite seasonal. Alaska Pops were made and distributed in spring, summer, and fall. Operations ceased in the winter months as demand waned. To no surprise, interest for gnawing on a frozen block of ice in January around here did not appeal to anyone.

Judy remembers one of the benefits of her family owned business. "When it was my birthday, I would bring a box of Alaska Pops to school! It was always a big hit with all the kids in my class."

On May 14, 1957, the Oshkosh Fire Department responded to a 3:53pm call at the popsicle shop located at 1319 Spruce Avenue. "My dad was out of town that day. As the firemen were working the scene, one of the firemen took an axe and walked toward the freezer. He was getting ready to bury the axe head into the freezer wall when my mother stepped in between the fireman and the freezer saying "No you don't! My husband built this freezer and you're not going to destroy it!" Judy was convinced that fireman was going to have to go through her mother if he wanted to get inside that freezer wall. It turned out to be an ammonia leak, no fire and structural damage was minimal. "My dad had the business running again by the very next day!" she exclaimed proudly.

I remember buying Alaska Pops for 2 for 5¢. Judy confirmed the price saying "Yes, that's right. Once my dad tried to raise the price to 3 for 10¢ but it raised so much commotion he couldn't do it."

Probably what made Alaska Pops seem so much better than their national competitor was the size, price, and flavor. Not only did you get a better value for your money, they tasted better too! "For the banana flavored pops we used real bananas" Judy stated.

When asked how the family could keep things going when they closed for the winter, she explained, "My dad's brother Chet ran a beer depot business out of the front part of store." A tactic I'm sure helped with the cost of maintaining the property.

In March 1958, Theophil "Phil" Nitkowski passed away unexpectedly at 7:30pm. According to his obituary, Nitkowski had been shoveling snow earlier in the day at the Frozen Products Company and upon feeling ill, returned home where he succumbed to a heart attack.

After his death, his wife Harriet continued to run the business with help from her family. Family friend, Lee Engleman, now Judy's husband, even pitched in and worked the deliveries at age seventeen. Judy told me "Mom no longer wanted to run the business. Lee would have liked to have taken it over, but at seventeen years old, he was too young."

The Nitkowskis sold the business in 1960 to Ira Farley of Neenah. Ira ran the business until 1963 when it was sold to H. Clifford Farley. During this ownership the company name was changed from Frozen Products Company to Alaska Pops Co. In 1968 the company changed hands one more time. James Oates of Appleton operated the frozen dessert company until it closed in 1975.

Today, you can still find popsicles in your grocer's freezer. But none compare to the Alaska Pops we enjoyed in the 1950s and 60s.

THE FROG FARMS

As it has been said many times in my writings and in those of other local authors, making a living in the early part of the twentieth century was not easy. At times, work was hard to find which meant people did what they could to take care of their families. My grandfather Clarence Ott was a "southsider" who worked at the Paine Lumber Company, and at one time made a little extra money recycling old clothing. He would take the items home, where my grandmother Agnes would wash the clothing and gather the kids around to cut the buttons off the garments. Once cleaned and free of buttons, the used clothing would be tied into bundles and sold as rags.

There are many examples of entrepreneurs who creatively found ways to scratch out a few extra bucks when times were hard.

One such venture that actually turned into a successful and thriving business was "frogging". "Froggers" is a term that is used to describe people who would hunt, catch, or raise various animals including frogs, turtles, worms, rabbits, lizards, snakes, clams, and just about anything else that swims, jumps, or crawls.

In this chapter, it is my sole intent to tell you everything you ever wanted to know about frogging…but were afraid to ask!

As a boy, I spent many summers at my uncle and aunt's cottage north of Oshkosh on Island Point. The cottage was surrounded by water, with Lake Winnebago on one side and a channel with marshlands on the other. We always took great pleasure in going from one stagnant water hole to another in search of pollywogs. When we did find some, we scooped them up and hurried home to find a goldfish bowl in which to keep them. Unsure if they were frogs or toads…we really didn't care! Each day we would check the bowl, inspecting the swimmers to see if they had sprouted any legs. And when they did appear, we were astounded! Eventually, my Aunt Loretta (Ziebell) would insist we take them across the street to the channel and release them. I think she was afraid once they had legs they would crawl out of the bowl and slither around the house. We released them reluctantly, but whenever we saw frogs, we couldn't help but wonder if they were from our pollywogs.

Also around that same time, family gatherings at the cottage would include a frogging expedition. Cousins, aunts, and uncles would be armed with makeshift frog spears which amounted to a stick with a finishing nail protruding from one end. The cottage was surrounded with tall grasses and the nearby lake, channel, and marshes provided a plentiful supply of Leopard frogs. Leopard frogs, also known as 'grass frogs', were common and usually green or brown with dark spots and smooth, slippery skin. They were champion jumpers so we called them "leapers".

Armed with our frog spears, our family waded into the grassy areas adjacent to the cottage and began spearing. What a sight it must have been to someone passing by. Shouting and laughter could be heard for blocks away. Once the days harvest was collected, the men would clean the frogs, skinning the legs, or saddles as they were called, and hand them off to the ladies who would bread and fry them. The feast was served with homemade french fries and a bottle of Pepsi Cola® for the kids, while the men washed them down with a couple bottles of ice cold Peoples® beer!

In the early 1900s, several local businesses were formed around frog farming. These were quite sizeable businesses at that. If you talked to a "frogger", they claimed to have never made any money in the frogging business. Nonetheless, it must have been profitable enough as several frog farms were doing business in Oshkosh in the early to mid 1900s.

In spite of the name, these businesses offerings included more than just frogs. Items like frog and turtle meat were sold to the restaurant industry, as frog legs were considered a delicacy by some and turtle meat made for some real tasty soup. Many Oshkosh taverns that sold food featured frog legs on their menu, usually along with fried lake perch and breaded shrimp. I recall going to Nigl's Chieftan in the 1960s and ordering frog legs. We would start by sitting at the bar with a beer and a friendly chat with "Punky" Nigl, who tended bar there for his brother "Porky". Ready to eat, we then moved to the room behind the bar and slid into a booth. Once we decided what we would have, we pressed the little white button on the wall. The button signaled the kitchen we were ready to order. Within seconds, Porky Nigl came out, towel draped across his shoulder, a white apron folded in half and neatly tied around his waist. He proceeded to put both hands on our table and lean in saying "What would you like?" Porky made eye contact with each person seated in the booth as they gave him their order. He never wrote anything down. Once finished, he turned and walked back to the kitchen. The perch and shrimp were delicious, but never as good as the frog legs. Food was served on a heavy paper plate. Takeout orders were plated the same but wrapped in the latest edition of the *Oshkosh Daily Northwestern* to keep your food hot until it arrived home.

In addition to the restaurant trade, many of the items sold were provided as specimens to schools, universities, and laboratories for teaching, research, and experimental purposes. Earthworms, preserved frogs and turtles, butterflies, garter snakes, clams, white rats were among the list of countless items available. You may even remember dissecting a frog in your high school biology class without giving a thought as to where they came from.

Frogs were easily found and in great supply in the early to mid 1900s. Countless marshes and bogs, that no longer exist today, provided what seemed like an endless supply. Over the years, frog supplies diminished due to over harvesting, causing the State of Wisconsin to step in and impose regulations.

During the depression era, frogs sold earned about five cents a pound. That was considered decent money for anyone willing to spend long hard days wading through marshlands, swamps, and creeks. Hip boots, dip nets, and a gunny sack were the uniform of the day for these weather worn outdoorsmen.

Local author Clarence "Inky" Jungwirth, in his book *A History of the City of Oshkosh, The Early Years, Volume 1*, points out some of the hazards "froggers" would face in the field. "They all had stories to tell about their run-ins with farmers and land-owners who on occasion would threaten them with shot guns over land and water rights." Inky continued to point out other "job related hazards" such as dealing with cantankerous snapping turtles where one careless mistake could mean the loss of a finger or two as you were feeling along the bottom of a stream bed for crayfish or clams.

William Lemberger

Photo Credit: Lemberger Company Catalogue
courtesy Steve Juedes

A book written by William Dawes and Clara Dawes in 1938 titled *History of Oshkosh* reports three such local frog businesses doing significant volume. The Lemberger family business was founded by Adolf and Frank Lemberger in 1919. Their business, which began mainly as a seller of bait frogs and frog legs, eventually expanded and became known as "a dealer in frogs, turtles, rabbits, grass hoppers, spiders, Guinea Pigs, frog eggs, snails, lizards, etc." From February to May in 1938, Lemberger reported over five tons of frogs were shipped (about 120,000 frogs) and 13,500 pounds of turtles (estimated to be about 1350 turtles as the average weight per turtle was about ten pounds. Turtles ranged in weight from about four to fifty pounds). Rabbits were also sold to restaurants and in just two months that year, Lemberger shipped 1000 tame rabbits to New York State.

Adolf's son, William, took over the business from his father and uncle around 1933. Local resident, Steve Juedes, remembers working for Lemberger as a teenager. "I worked for Bill from 1966 until 1972. I started when I was 15 years old and earned a wage of ninety cents per hour," he said with a grin. Steve related all the different jobs he performed over the years working in the business. "I drove delivery trucks, worked in the plant processing frogs and turtles mostly, you name it. If there was a job to be done and I was told to do it…I did it," he said. Lemberger had a good business locally selling frog legs to the taverns and restaurants. "Frank Nachtman would dress the frog legs, I would pack and refrigerate them, then deliver same day to places like Nigl's Chieftin on Ninth Ave and Ohio Street. They were one of our biggest frog leg customers in the area," Steve said.

Nigl's Chieftin on Ninth St. and Ohio featured frog legs on their menu (Note sign in window on right).

Photo Credit: Dan Radig

But most of the specimens Steve worked with were designated for biological studies. A biological application of live frogs was developed as a test to determine early pregnancy. Live male frogs were used and the test was deemed to be 99.5% accurate. Testing did not harm the frog allowing them to be used many times over. Other scientific uses did not require the use of live specimens. "We would prepare the frogs by euthanizing them first, then injecting them with formaldehyde. The specimens were then placed carefully inside a barrel in a stretched out fashion. Most of the specimens were used for research and teaching biology students," he recalled.

Lemberger operated his business from two locations. The "shop", where all the processing, receiving, and shipping took place, was located at 1402 South Park Ave (current address 1152 South Park Ave). A second facility was built near Rush Lake where live frogs, turtles, and occasionally salamanders where kept in cement pens filled with fresh spring water. "Frogs were separated by date of receipt so we always knew the fresh arrivals from those earlier," Steve explained. "The water we used was from an artesian well. It was crystal clear which was good for keeping the specimens alive and well." About twice weekly, depending on volume, Steve transported frogs and turtles in crates and nylon bags from the Oshkosh shop to the Rush Lake holding facility in one of Lemberger's delivery trucks.

One of Steve's first jobs at age fifteen was preserving crawfish. He described the process of injecting the little Cajun critters with formaldehyde, then placing them in a 55 gallon drum for shipment. "They were intended for biological use and we shipped worldwide. A drum would hold about 2,000 crayfish," he added.

Another job was known as "pegging clams". Steve described the technique. A small knife-like blade was inserted near the hinge holding the two shell halves together. A little twist of the blade allowed the shell to open just wide enough to insert a small wooden peg. The force of the clam trying to keep its shell closed held the peg in place. When asked why clams were pegged, Steve replied, "That allowed the preserving fluids to get inside the clam." He remembers pegging about 2,000 clams a day. They too were a specimen sold for science. "Shorty" Frank 'clammed' almost every day in the Embarrass River near Pella, Wisconsin. He then mused, "He would bring in 1,000 to 2,000 clams each day." Steve then got a bit serious. "You know, we did a lot of things in those days that are no longer acceptable practices. It's illegal to harvest or sell clams today as they are considered a protected species." It was a time before regulatory laws were put in place to prevent over harvesting of many animals including frogs, turtles, and other natural resources.

In the late fall, when the weather turned cold, frogs would gather together on the lake bottoms in preparation for their winter hibernation. "Froggers would chop holes in the ice and 'dip net' the bottom. When they did find the huddled up frogs, they were to be had in good numbers" Steve remembered.

Turtles were also a big business for most "froggers" back then and processing them required a special skill and technique. "I became pretty good at cleaning snappers," Steve said. He remembers a few guys who knew the tricks of the trade and could clean a turtle in no time. "Binx" Hannes and Dennis Hannes were two men Steve remembered who were very skilled. Local meat cutter Ralph Schaetz also moonlighted from his meat cutting job at Buehler Brothers to clean turtles on evenings and weekends. Once cleaned, the turtle meat was divided and sold by parts – tails, legs, and backs. "We would pack and freeze turtle meat until we had enough to fill a semi trailer," Steve explained. "Much of what we sold was sent to Campbell's Soup® in Chicago" he recalled. We both tried in vain to remember seeing a can of Campbell's Turtle Soup on the grocery store shelves. "I'm not sure exactly what it was used for," he finished with a chuckle.

One of the easiest money making opportunities for a young boy was collecting earthworms. "We'd ride our bikes over to the Southside Lighted Baseball Diamond on Sawyer Street after a rain in the evening. It was a gold mine for worms. We got a penny apiece but if you picked a couple hundred that was good money to a kid," Steve recalled.

Not all the specimens collected and sold were caught locally. "Frogs came in from all over. Brownsville Texas was a big source, as were North Dakota and Minnesota. We even bought frogs from Mexico and Manitoba," Steve informed me. "Bill Lemberger would get a call from Brownsville, Texas saying they had a ton a frogs. So Jacob "Jack" Gonia, who was also employed by Lemberger, would drive there and pick them up."

The local froggers were a bunch of guys who learned the trade and converted the skill of finding and catching frogs into a decent source of income. Steve remembers them well. "It was always the same guys who caught and sold frogs and turtles." As he started to name them, he added "They were known in the trade as "Pirates", but once you knew them, they were the nicest bunch of fellows. Some were a little rough around the edges but they were always nice to me." It seemed like everyone had a nickname. "Coonie" (John) Kloiber, "Shorty" (Leonard) Frank, brothers "Squeege and Nucky" Nachtman and "Binx" Hannes just to name a few. Skooner Robl was good at catching snakes. Steve recalled traveling to North Dakota one fall with Robl. "In the fall, snakes will gather underground and form a "snake ball", and that's how they spend the winter in hibernation. It was like Robl had a sixth sense. He knew exactly when to be there when the snakes were gathering. We'd sit on the ground and wait near the areas he knew the snakes would be going. Sure enough, after awhile, snakes would come crawling. We wore long leather gloves and caught them by hand, placing them in a large gunny sack."

These men all had special locations where they knew good supplies of whatever they were hunting existed. "It was a very secretive business," Steve said. "You didn't breathe a word where you were going or what you were catching." Sometimes word would leak out and guys would compete for "unauthorized rights" on lands that were either public or privately owned.

Steve remembers "Coonie" Kloiber died while frogging around Plainfield. "He was my uncle and was the person who landed me the job at Lembergers when I was 15. He had a heart attack. "Shorty" Frank also died in the field near Weyauwega. When "Shorty" and "Coonie" went out for the day, they always told each other where they were going. One day "Shorty" wasn't back and it was well after the usual time, so my Uncle "Coonie" went out looking for him and found him dead. Kloiber and Frank both died doing what they loved."

In Lembergers' 50th Anniversary Catalog published in 1969, the company reported providing live frogs to NASA for experimental purposes on Gemini 8 and Gemini 12 missions. Among the hundreds of specimens available, Lemberger listed fetal pigs in his catalog. The unborn fetal pigs were purchased from Oscar Mayer in Madison where they had a fresh pork processing facility.

Bill Lemberger sold his business in 1970 to another Oshkosh company, Mogul-ED, – another biological supply business. Lemberger died on Easter Sunday, April 7, 1996 in Ontario, California. He was 81 years of age and is buried in Oshkosh's Sacred Heart Cemetery.

E.G. Hoffman ran his frog business about this same time from 949 Florida Street. Hoffman dealt in many of the same items as Lemberger and reported he sold about 24,000 frogs and 1000 pounds of turtle each week during the spring and fall, most of which was sold to restaurants on the east coast. Hoffman also provided small frogs to bait shops where they were used extensively as Black Bass bait.

E.R. Neuenfeldt started in the frogging business at his home on Seventh Avenue near what today is Sawyer Avenue. Part of Neuenfeldt's success stemmed from selling frogs for fishing bait. "Inky" Jungwirth wrote that Neuenfeldt started out as a newsboy on the Wisconsin Central Railroad. While making his rounds on the train, men would ask him where they could buy fishing bait. The young Neuenfeldt started selling frogs and other fishing bait to the travelers at the train stop and began what turned into a "very brisk business". Eventually, Neuenfeldt and the Railroad worked out a deal and sold his frogs through the railroad company.

A newspaper article from the *Crawford County Democrat*, English, Indiana, reported Neuenfeldt had leased a thousand acre farm near Lomira, Wisconsin to raise frogs. The April 9, 1903 article titled ***"Raising Frogs By The Millions For Market"*** stated the farm was leased from a well known member of the Milwaukee Chamber of Commerce named John Buerger.

> *Neuenfeldt, of Oshkosh,...will convert it into the greatest frog preserve in the Northwest. Mr. Neuenfeldt will use five picturesque lakes upon the farm for his frog project. The ponds, which were formerly the finest trout ponds in the State, will be cleaned out and devoted to the raising of frogs of all kinds and descriptions, from the very small variety used to entice gamey bass to the larger species whose hind legs are used by the thousands in the spring and summer months in all the large hotels in the West, and by people who recognize frogs' legs as a choice table delicacy.*

The article, which refers to Mr. Neuenfeldt as "the J. Pierpoint Morgan" of the frog industry, goes on to explain about his plans to diversify.

> *Mr. Neuenfeldt by no means intends to confine himself to the frog industry, as he has planned to raise horned toads by wholesale. The horned toad has usually been considered an adornment for a curiosity cabinet, but Mr. Neuenfeldt has discovered a practical use for this product of the desert. "Among the side issues that I propose to establish with my frog farm," says Mr. Neuenfeldt, "is a distribution agency for horned toads. This species of reptile lives mostly in the deserts of this country, and their great value is in destroying bugs such as infest and ruin fine flower beds. I will also raise all kinds of turtles, crawfish, mussels, edible snails. Insects and worms, to be kept to supply the growing demand for educational institutions throughout the country.*

The article then delves into a very interesting perspective by Neuenfeldt on how frogs are raised.

Mr. Neuenfeldt's Oshkosh plant consists of a ten-acre pond adjoining Lake Butte des Morts, three miles from Oshkosh. The land adjoining the lake is both high and low, with a ridge along the lakeside and a dam is to be placed along the lower end of this body of ground, while a windmill will throw water from the lake over the ridge at the upper end. This will create an artificial pond and marsh, insuring continuous fresh water and at a proper temperature. A dam is necessary for the control of the water, because water is not essential for the growth of the frog at a certain season of the year, and because at other seasons it must be kept high enough to protect the spawn until the sun develops it into the pollywog and then into the next grade, the tadpole. In their wild state millions of frogs are destroyed annually because the water lowers so rapidly that the spawn is left on high ground. Instead of being developed by the sun the spawn becomes food for reptiles, turtles and fish. The artificial pond and marsh which Mr. Neuenfeldt will establish will thus be a protection to the infantile frogs against fish and turtles, while a high boarded fence about it will prevent the insidious snake from creeping into the home of the frog, thus saving thousands of frogs' legs for the tables of epicures. Upon the subject of preparing frogs for the market and as a table delicacy, Mr. Neuenfeldt says: "Frogs are a selling commodity in all stores, and the wise business man who keeps a sporting goods establishment is never without them. Frogs legs are a dainty food for anybody and they are especially beneficial to the sick and the invalid. They are not enjoyed as they should be because they are not properly handled. Frog's legs at their best should be on the table twelve hours after they are dressed. Now the catcher kills them and drags them along for a day prepares them for the market the next day after, and are placed on the market for sale or put in cold storage for future use, and by the time they reach the table they have lost their nourishment and richness of flavor. The proper way is to obtain them alive, solicit your order and dress them accordingly. If they are on the bill for dinner in Milwaukee, they are dressed at 6 a. m. in Oshkosh and properly prepared for the table. This plan obtained favor with my patrons from the start."

According to the *Oshkosh Daily Northwestern*, the article ran in the Indiana paper was previously reported in a Milwaukee newspaper which caused a rebuttal to be printed that same year.

Mrs. E. Neuenfeldt, the young man's mother, states the story is all wind...Mr. Neuenfeldt sells frogs, but he has no farm. He operates a small shanty near the Wisconsin Central round house on Fourth Street where he keeps the frogs he buys. He has talked of leasing a small ten-acre piece of land near the city and going into the frog raising business, but has not yet done so, nor has he leased a 1,000 acre farm at Lomira.

According to his obituary in the June 18, 1954 edition of the *Oshkosh Daily Northwestern*, Neuenfeldt's business began in 1904 and listed him as operating "the first frog farm in this vicinity." It went on to say he left Oshkosh in 1927 and moved to Windsor, Canada (near Detroit), then moved to Champlain, New York ten years later. He continued to operate frog farms in both locations. He was "about" 78 years old at the time of his death.

Elmer G. Steinhilber.
Photo Credit: Wisconsin
Magazine, December 1950

Elmer G. Steinhilber was the "frogger" I remember best. His business was located on the west side of town, close to Campbell Creek on Josslyn Avenue, not far from Lourdes High School. In 1938, it was reported Steinhilber employed ten men and many free-lancers who combed the rivers, marshes and forest for specimens. Steinhilber's tanks could accommodate 250,000 frogs. He also sold cats for experimental research when it was still legal to do so. "Cats are used in the fight against syphilis and rabbits in checking for Rocky Mountain spotted fever" Steinhilber stated.

Steinhilber gained unwanted publicity in 1952 when he was charged with shipping cats out of state for experimental purposes. An article in the June 16, 1952 edition of the *Oshkosh Daily Northwestern* reported:

The complaint read today charged him with sending "outside the State of Wisconsin, from Oshkosh to the University of Chicago, two crates of four living cats in each to be used for medical, surgical and chemical investigation, experiment and demonstration."

The article goes on to explain that the complaint was filed by the Animal Protective Association, with the Winnebago County Humane Society in attendance as spectators, assisting the APA. In his defense, Steinhilber stated "he had been expecting it" and that "his firm has been furnishing small laboratories for the past 30 years and he had commitments to take care of with atomic and cancer research groups." An investigator for the APA reported all eight of the cats were recovered and safely returned to their rightful owners.

Steinhilber pleaded "not guilty" and the case was scheduled to go to trial on July 29, 1952 when Municipal Court Judge S. J. Luchsinger ruled the Wisconsin Statute prohibiting the shipment of domestic animals was unconstitutional. Steinhilber's attorney, Henry P. Hughes, a former State Supreme Court Justice, said the statute violated the Constitution by prohibiting interstate commerce. The case was then dismissed by Judge Luchsinger.

As the years went by, the frog industry did not go unnoticed. In 1963, Sports Illustrated did a feature story on frogs in their April 1st edition, and the article even mentioned Oshkosh's E.G. Steinhilber. The article reports Steinhilber sold one-and-a-half million frogs in 1962, a record year for the Oshkosh "frogger". Between 400 and 500 "hunters" supplied the enormous numbers that year. Retail prices for live grass frogs were 95 cents to $5 a dozen depending on size. Jumbo bullfrogs could be as large as three pounds would fetch as much as $3 apiece.

Culinary experts claim the smaller legs are highly prized and preferred over the jumbo, meatier ones. So, the next time you are in your favorite restaurant and see frog legs on the menu, give them a try. Or if you are more the adventurous type, go and round up a mess of frogs, clean them (or just order them from your local seafood supplier) and try this recipe:

Frog Legs in Batter (serves four)
24 small or 16 medium pairs of frog's legs, soaked in 1 ¼ cup milk
BATTER:
1 cup plus 2 tbsp all-purpose flour
½ tsp salt
2 eggs
1 cup milk
1 tbsp corn or vegetable oil

Soak frog's legs in milk for 30-60 minutes. Combine flour and salt in a bowl. Beat slightly 1 whole egg plus yolk and mix with 1 cup milk. Gradually stir until smooth. Add oil. Just before using, fold in the remaining egg white, beaten until it holds a point. The batter should have the consistency of heavy cream, if it appears too thick, add a little more milk.

Pat frog's legs dry and dip into batter. Shake off excess batter and fry in deep fat previously heated to 370 °. Do not use deep fry basket. Fry for 3-4 minutes until crust is golden brown. Drain on paper towels. Frog legs can be served with your favorite tartar sauce but tastes best when served only with lemon wedges. Serves four.

The industry began to fade after World War II. The widespread use of pesticides in farming began to have a dramatic impact on supplies. Disappearing habitat occurred with the filling in of wet-lands and expansion of residential development into the rural areas. Additionally, state and local legislation imposed restrictions on many species to protect against overharvesting, making it more difficult to earn a living collecting specimens.

As that generation of "froggers" have aged and passed, no one is waiting in line to take their place. The stories and memories of "Nucky", "Coonie", "Shorty", "Squeege", "Binx", "Skooner", "Tuffy", "Schnous" and the others only remain as tales for their family members and those who knew them.

If by now I have not given you all of the information you needed to know about the frog business, you can pick up a copy of the book *Frog Raising For Profit and Pleasure* by Dr. Albert Broel.

(Sources: The History of Oshkosh, William Dawes, Clara Dawes; A History Of The City Of Oshkosh, The Early Years, Clarence J. Jungwirth; *Oshkosh Daily Northwestern*, June 16, 1952, June 12, 1952, August 25, 1952, November 1, 1952, November 14, 1952, April 8, 1996; SIVault April 1, 1963, The Milwaukee Journal, January 11, 1972)

LITTLE BASTARD

N ow, before you slap a PG13 rating on this chapter, let me explain.

The story I am about to share with you involves an Oshkosh man who has achieved not only one, but two professional careers—one as a professional wrestler; the other a professional actor. But let me start at the beginning.

Dylan Postl was born on May 29, 1986. The son of Eric and Terry Postl is different than others, but only in stature. He is a little person. Dylan's parents were estranged early in his life and he was raised in a family that included a stepmother and two stepbrothers, Tim and Ben. Dylan was raised by his father, Eric Postl, and his only natural brother, Clint, died at the early age of 16 years. His grandfather, Forrest Postl was also a big influence in Dylan's formative years. "My dad has always been my biggest supporter...he was always there when I needed him. He was instrumental in helping me become what I am today...not only in my professional career, but also that of a father." Dylan is now a father as well and his son Landon, who is four years old as of this writing, is his pride and joy.

I met Dylan for lunch one day in September of 2014. Until recently, I didn't know of Dylan or of his accomplishments, but came quickly up to speed by "Google-ing" his name. I was anxious to meet this young man who at the age of 28 had carved out a very successful career as a professional wrestler with the WWE and even starred in two recent movies. I surmised that many local residents were also unaware of this man and his accomplishments, so I decided this was a story that was worth telling.

Dylan Postl, 2014
photo credit: Randy Domer

We shared some introductory conversation over lunch, then turned on my tape recorder and started the interview.

"I've spent my entire childhood life here in Oshkosh. It's my home and most likely will always be my home." He described Oshkosh as "a small town that didn't want to be a big town...it just feels like home" as one of his reasons for staying here. He also is proud of his close relationship with his dad. "He doesn't always agree with my decisions but remains supportive. He'll tell me when he thinks I'm making a mistake, but that's what Dads are supposed to do. I live my life to make him proud."

Even as a young child, Dylan loved wrestling. "I used to watch it with my Grandpa Postl. When I was six years old I used to tell him "...someday I'm going to be a wrestler." His dad encouraged him to go to college. "I did but I flunked four of the six classes I attended. I even flunked choir!" he said rather amused with himself. But college was not what Dylan had in mind. His lifelong dream to become a professional wrestler never diminished. "I knew I wanted to be a wrestler, so I quit college and much to my dad's dismay, started pursuing my dream. I always knew when one of my dad's famous lectures was coming when he started with 'I know you don't want to hear this Dylan...', but I now know, as a dad, I will do the same thing with my son."

As he started to unravel his life for me, he mentioned the numerous tattoos that I could clearly see on his arms. "I have over 50 tattoos," he exclaimed. "I love them. They are an art form. Almost every one represents something important in my life." He started to describe several that were most important to him and informed me his legs and back were also covered with symbolic images. "I have a leg full of *Muppets®*! I've always been a Muppet fanatic. I started with Animal and Kermit, then just kept going. When the Muppets guest starred on

WWE, they knew about my tattoos and were just as excited to meet me as I was them." He then explained he has what he calls his "family arm". "It illustrates things that relate to my family and my childhood. I also have the Oshkosh skyline on that arm as well". He continued "The 4 G's symbolizes the four generations of Postl men...my grandfather, dad, myself and my son Landon." Across his chest are the words "Can't Bring Me Down". Dylan explained it is a reminder that every time he's been told he couldn't do something, he has risen and accomplished his goal. He then concluded by saying, "The one that is most meaningful to me are Landon's handprints on my back. It is a constant reminder that he is always with me." The tattoos are very special to Dylan. "They are who I am".

On his journey to fame, Dylan was faced with some serious obstacles. He had back surgery that paralyzed him. Follow up surgeries were performed to try to restore use of his body. "On the second surgery, they removed one of my ribs and fused a metal rod in my back. I was in a full body cast and had to teach myself how to walk all over again." He added, "The doctor said no contact sports and no stressful activities like trampolines. A few years later that same doctor saw me on WWE and called my dad to say 'well, I can see he didn't listen to me'."

I asked Dylan to tell me how his professional wrestling career began. One night, a young Dylan and his friends attended a local wrestling promotion in Oshkosh. "After the performance, I approached a man named Ken Anderson and asked how I could pursue a career in wrestling. He put me in touch with the people from the Wisconsin group of wrestling and I started training to become a professional wrestler."

In 2005, Dylan had made it to the Independents circuit, considered to be wrestling's minor league system in Wisconsin and the Midwest. Realizing the need to be noticed, Dylan worked to create his own niche in professional wrestling. His first professional name was **Shortstack: The World's Sexiest Midget**. The early years meant working small town venues like bars, high school gymnasiums, and National Guard armories to hone his skills. But it was small price to pay to learn the tools of the trade.

The move to become a wrestler wasn't driven by money. "I made $20 a show when I started out. Sometimes we would do two shows a week and made $40."

But grass didn't grow under Dylan's feet. Only one year later his phone rang and along with it came a new opportunity. "Mr. Kennedy called me and said WWE was looking for someone new and they wanted me." Stunned at the news, Postl accepted the invitation to try-out and immediately was offered a contract. At 19 years of age, he had made the big time.

Now that he had reached the pinnacle of the sport, a new identity needed to be created to introduce this new phenom to rabid wrestling fans worldwide. "A wrestling commentator referred to me one time as *Little Bastard* and it stuck!" Dylan said with a sly grin. "The name only survived a short while though, once they realized it was a difficult name to market publicly."

Dylan's television debut came on May 26, 2006 on WWE's *SmackDown!* Playing the role of leprechaun partner to fellow Irish wrestler Finlay, *Little Bastard* was portrayed as an extremely hyper, mysterious little man in a leprechaun costume who would scurry out from under the ring, laughing maniacally while attacking his partner's foe.

In 2007 after much consideration, *Little Bastard* became *Hornswoggle*. The name was perfect for the role Dylan had developed as the definition of hornswoggle is 'to cheat or swindle'. Hornswoggle quickly became a fan favorite, in spite of playing the role of "bad guy" in the ring. In 2007, Hornswoggle won the WWE Cruiserweight title by pinning Jamie Noble, earning the coveted championship belt. He would be the last wrestler to win the coveted award as the title was retired after that season. Noble contested the decision and the following week the two squared off again on *SmackDown!* Hornswoggle defended his title by defeating Noble once again, this time by count out. His feud with Noble continued that season as Hornswoggle's attack strategy included throwing a pie in his face and spraying him with a fire extinguisher.

Dylan decided to share a story with me that illustrated the humorous side of his storied wrestling career. "My first Riding Team with WWE included myself standing in at four-foot four; a Arab-American named Shawn Daivari; at seven-foot one The Great Kahli from India (also known as the Punjabi Giant); and an enormous African American man, Mark Henry, who at 6'4" tips the scales at over 400 lbs. and claims to be the World's Strongest Man! Picture the four of us crammed into a van for six months. It was my first riding tour and we were a sight to behold," he said with a laugh. "You should've seen the looks on the peoples' faces when the four of us walked into a Denny's® or IHOP®!" The Great Kahli didn't speak a lick of English so Daivari would speak with him in Hindu. Dylan was amused as he recalled an incident from those early days. "One day we were driving along and we were pulled over by police. When the officer approached the vehicle Mark Henry, the huge, African American strongman opened the door of the van. When the officer peered inside and saw the four of us, he didn't know what to say...he was speechless! We were like a traveling circus....a bunch of misfits." Then he continued, "But that was my family. We spent more time together on the road than we did with our own families. We were very close."

One day in 2011, WWE approached Dylan about an idea to do a movie, a sequel of sort with the Leprechaun franchise. It made sense to Dylan that the person who played the Leprechaun on WWE would be the one to play the Leprechaun in the movie. Two years went by but nothing ever developed on the idea.

It was about this same time the opportunity for Dylan to play a big role in a new Muppets movie came about. "I have always been a HUGE Muppets fan my entire life so I jumped at the chance to take the role. The Muppets had done a couple of guest appearances on WWE Raw and the Tribute to the Troops Show, so Dylan had become familiar with some of the Muppets performers and staff. When Dylan heard the Muppets were planning to do a new film, he became excited. "I was giddy at the idea of doing that gig, so I met with the team at WWE and proposed the idea. WWE and Disney met and agreed to offer me a cameo role in the movie." Originally the cameo was intended to be one scene, but was later expanded. "I played a prisoner in a Russian Gulag," Dylan said with a grin. "They wanted me to use a Russian accent but once they heard how bad I was, they decided to go without it." He went on to describe what a thrill it was to work with co-stars Tina Fey, Danny Trejo, Ray Liotta, Ricky Gervais, and Ty Burrell. *Muppets Most Wanted* was filmed in London, and as this was Postl's first role in films, he had much to learn. "With the Muppets, I learned to always look the character in the eyes, never down at the hand that brings the Muppet to life."

During the filming of *Muppets Most Wanted*, Dylan called home from London to find his son, Landon, was sick. Realizing that he was in a very unique situation being surrounded by some of the most famous stars in the world... Kermit, Miss Piggy and cast, Dylan came up with a marvelous idea. "My son is like me and watches the Muppets on TV every chance he gets. His favorite Muppet character is Animal." So Dylan approached the performer who brings Animal to life and asked a big, big favor. Later that day, back in Oshkosh, a Facetime call came into Landon Postl. It was Animal himself! He was calling to ask Landon how he was feeling and wished him well, telling him to get better soon. Shortly after the call ended, Dylan's phone rang. "Dad! Guess what?!!! Animal called me!" It was a moment young Landon Postl will remember for a lifetime.

Upon completion of the Muppets film, the Leprechaun project assumed new life and in 2013filming on Dylan's next movie began. Dylan talked about his role in *Leprechaun: Origins*. "The leprechaun character was "gollum-esque" (referring to the evil Gollum of *Lord of the Rings* fame) which required me to spend two-and-one half hours in the makeup chair twice a day." *Leprechaun: Origins* was filmed in Vancouver that summer. "That summer was a scorcher, even reaching temperatures of over a hundred degrees Fahrenheit one day. It was so hot and extremely uncomfortable with all the make-up and prosthetics. Once I was in character, I couldn't even eat, just drink through a straw." Postl explained. The suit and costume weighed 25 pounds adding to the discomfort.

As Dylan reflected on his two movie roles, he stated he has so much to be grateful for. "I never dreamed of being an actor. Here I am just a kid from small-town Oshkosh...a kid who never should've made it. I've gone further than I ever dreamed. It's unbelievable!" He finished his thought by joking that acting was much easier on the body than wrestling.

There is also the side of professional wrestlers that the public seldom sees. Dylan talked about his best friend and fellow WWE superstar John Cena. "John is very much involved with the Make-A-Wish Foundation. Last year he did over three hundred Make-A-Wish appearances." Dylan's words then softened as he shared an experience he had with a Make-A-Wish child. "First, I was amazed that the child wanted to meet me...me! Of all the people he could've requested, he wanted to meet me...a small town guy from Oshkosh, Wisconsin. What was supposed to be a brief meeting turned into a two-hour event. I didn't want to leave."

Today, Dylan is still active with WWE as Hornswoggle and looking to advance his career in the wrestling arena. He has wrestled on every continent but two – Africa and Antarctica. "I've wrestled in Australia, the Philippines, even football stadiums in front of 80,000 people!" he stated with a tone of self-amazement. He has numerous "action figures" done in his likeness and if you would like to see him in action, go to YouTube and type in the keyword "Hornswoggle".

With two Pay-Per-View matches from 2014 under his belt, he has both the experience and popularity to sustain his professional wrestling career. He also plans to write a book. "I think I have one hell of a story to tell."

THE BUBBLER

"**I**f you're thirsty, go get a drink out of the bubbler!"

Those of us who grew up in Oshkosh and around Wisconsin only knew drinking water fountains as *bubblers* and nothing else.   Schools all had bubblers as did most public places around Wisconsin. Travel outside Wisconsin and mention the name "bubbler" and you will get the oddest looks from people... "What's a bubbler?"

It turns out there is a good explanation for this.

Water fountains have been around for a long time. Back in 1889, a man named Harlan Huckleby designed the very first bubbler. The design was unique to other drinking fountains as it had a spout of water which shot up about an inch or so into the air allowing people to drink without a cup. The new fixture was obtained and patented by a company known then as Kohler Water Works, which today we all know as the internationally famous Kohler Company of Kohler Wisconsin. To promote and market this new plumbing device, Kohler trademarked and named it "*The Bubbler*®." The name *Bubbler* became synonymous with drinking fountains around Wisconsin the same as other brands like *JELL-O*™, *Band-Aid*™ and *Popsicle* ™.

The original design had about a one-inch stream of water shooting straight up in the air. Concerns from local health departments that the process was unsanitary were raised because as one was drinking, water touching their mouth was falling back down onto the faucet nozzle creating the possibility of contamination and spreading contagious diseases. The design was soon modified to have the water arc slightly alleviating health concerns.

Although still commonly used in Wisconsin, the term bubbler today is also used in some states in the eastern US and as far away as Australia. The Encarta online dictionary defines the word 'bubbler' as: *(noun), a drinking fountain, especially one that spouts water from a vertical nozzle*

In Portland, Oregon a logging magnate named Simon Benson grew tired of his loggers drinking alcohol to excess and wanted a solution. Simon decided to offer an alternative by installing a number of continuous running water fountains throughout the city. Benson made a donation of $10,000 to the city of Portland in 1912 to cover the cost of installing twenty fountains. The *Benson Bubblers,* as they were soon to be known, were constructed from bronze and originally cost $500 to cast. Over the years, the *Benson Bubblers* fell into disrepair and the city reduced some of the four-bowl shaped fountains to two bowls. It was felt the *Benson Bubblers* were a key part of Portland's rich heritage and in 1958 a restoration effort was formed and the city refurbished sixteen of the original fountains and re-cast four others. [1]

Back home in Wisconsin, some of the original bubblers can still be found today near the Capitol building in Madison. You can even install one in your home. Featured in the Kohler catalogue of plumbing fixtures, a polished chrome-finished *Bubbler®* can be purchased for around $230.

[1] Source: www.Oregonencyclopedia.org

THE LARSON BROTHERS AIRPORT

I f you've lived around Oshkosh anytime over the past forty plus years or so, you will certainly know that Oshkosh is known internationally as the location of one of the biggest aviation events in the world. The EAA (Experimental Aircraft Association) fly-in, AirVenture, is an annual event that makes its home here each summer.

The EAA was formed in 1953 in Milwaukee by Wisconsin native Paul Poberezny and originally organized to aid and assist amateur aircraft builders. However, its purposes quickly encompassed the promotion of all facets of recreational aviation and the promotion of aviation safety.

That same year, the first annual EAA Fly-In Convention was held at Curtiss-Wright Airport (today known as Timmerman Field) in Milwaukee, with 21 aircraft and about 150 people attending. In 1970, Poberezny was instrumental in moving the convention to Oshkosh where it has thrived and grown. The *Oshkosh Northwestern* recently reported between 300,000 and 500,000 attendees gather each year for the weeklong convention, and the EAA website estimates approximately 10,000 planes will arrive at Oshkosh's Wittman Regional Airport for the event.

But the EAA is not the only organization to put this area on the map in aviation history.

Nestled peacefully in a quiet little farming community in northwest Winnebago County is a place where early aviation history began in Wisconsin. In 1922, four brothers from a local farming family had a growing interest in aviation. Because aviation was still in its infancy, airports and landing areas had not yet been established this far north of

Milwaukee. It was here and then, the Larson Brothers decided to build an airstrip. Roy Larson and his three younger brothers Clarence, Newell and Leonard worked to build their own landing strip which would become known as one of the first airports in the state outside Milwaukee.

Roy Larson, the eldest of five sons born to Charles and Julia Larson, had just returned from war in 1919. The war had changed Roy in many ways...one being his passion to someday fly. During the war, Roy marveled at the flying machines soaring overhead in France, dreaming someday it would be him up there. Shortly after arriving home from war, Roy shared his dream with his brothers. Clarence, Newell and young Leonard listened in awe as Roy described his plan that included taking flying lessons, buy a plane, and build a hangar and an airstrip. Funds could be earned by giving flying lessons and rides...maybe take aerial photos to sell to people and business. "We will be known as The Flying Larson Brothers!" Roy exclaimed.

It was obvious Roy had things pretty well thought out...except for one thing. His mother was not in favor of him flying...not one bit. She reminded Roy there was a farm to take care of and made him promise he wouldn't fly. Her son George's health was failing quickly from the effects tuberculosis and Roy's only sister, Zola had recently started showing the same symptoms. Julia Larson knew she may lose two of her dear children and would not be able to bear the loss of another flying those dangerous flying machines. Roy's promise to his mother was that "...she would never see him fly". In Roy's mind, he reasoned "that doesn't mean I won't fly."

In the summer of 1920, Roy could no longer control his urge to fly. Telling his family he was going to Milwaukee to attend the State Fair, he secretly drove to Chicago to the Diggins Flying School where he took flying lessons. Later that year, tragedy struck the Larson family. George finally succumbed to tuberculosis and died. About a year later, Roy's only sister, Zola, also died from TB at the very young age of seventeen. Losing two of her children within a year was too much for mother Julia, who worked so hard to keep the family and farm going. Julia died from a stroke on April 22, 1922, leaving behind her sons Roy, Clarence, Newell and Leonard to take care of the farm and each other.

Not long after Julia's death, Roy felt his obligation to his mother had been relinquished. He traveled to Duluth and purchased his first plane; a Curtiss Canuck, a Canadian built model of the American JN4 or "Jenny". Later that summer he acquired two more planes. Known as Standard J-1 bi-planes, they arrived at the Larson farm on December 22, 1922.

That winter was unusually cold and it helped hasten Roy's plan to build a hangar to store and work on his planes. But that would have to wait as another tragedy soon struck the Larson family. A fire completely destroyed the home that Charles Larson purchased in 1900. The two-story home was heated with a wood stove that created a chimney fire in the attic, quickly setting the entire house ablaze. The boys all escaped unharmed but were unable to salvage more than a few sparse belongings. With the help of friends and neighbors, the boys built a new home in January of 1923.

By the spring of 1924, work began to build a new hangar. Roy Larson needed a place to store the aircraft he had recently purchased and protect them from severe wind and weather. He also needed a place to build and repair planes and do mechanical work. Roy decided to use his army discharge money to buy some marshland timber from neighbor Charlie Lea to build a hangar. The new structure would hold up to six airplanes and give the Larson brothers some room to work. The site for the hangar was selected on a piece of ground that was slightly higher than the surrounding area.

Roy then decided to clear an 80 rod long sod landing strip behind their barn located just east of Winchester in the Town of Clayton. To further their knowledge on how to build and maintain these new flying machines, Roy and his brother Clarence attended the Sweeney Mechanics School in Kansas City, Missouri. Then, as promised, Roy taught his brothers how to fly.

In the spring of 2014, I had the privilege to meet the daughter of Leonard Larson and was invited to her home to talk about those early days in aviation history. Theda Eckstein lives on a farm, adjacent to the original family farm which holds the historic hanger and sod landing strip. Local resident and historian Peter Christensen knew the Ecksteins and arranged the meeting one evening in May.

We arrived at the Eckstein home around six o'clock in the evening and found Theda waiting for us seated in her living room. She greeted us with a warm smile and invited us into her home. Joining Theda (pronounced *thee'-dah,* as she corrected me) was her husband Abe Eckstein and grandson Ben Joas. I could tell immediately they were anxious to tell the story of their family's wonderful history in flying. Lying on the coffee table was a thick scrapbook or album that piqued my curiosity. As I looked around the living room I saw framed paintings of aviation and a large wooden propeller mounted over the doorway that led to the rest of the house…truly the setting of a family that grew up around aviation. I asked Theda about the propeller and where it came from. "Oh, I'm not sure," she replied looking up at it. "It's been in our house as long as I can remember."

At 79 years young, Theda was vibrant and anxious to talk about her famous flying family. Her voice was a bit frail and at times it was difficult for her to speak. But Abe and Ben were at the ready and very helpful filling in the blanks and explaining things when needed.

"When Roy bought that first plane in 1922, they had to remove the wings so they could store the plane in the barn that first winter" she said with a smile. Abe added "They put the wings up in the hay mow and the fuselage back in the shed. Then they built the hangar in 1924, cutting the wood from nearby land employing the assistance of a local barn builder named Knute Johnson to help build it." The hangar measured 52 ft by 60 ft. Theda remembers her father, Leonard, telling her how he helped build the new hanger. "His job was to hand-drill the holes in the main beams for pegging".

Larson Brothers hangar circa 1920s

Photo credit: Ben Joas and Theda Eckstein

Abe then explained "Leonard told us that shortly after that, their mother died...and Roy bought an airplane." Abe continued, then added "Then he bought two more! I think it might have been his plan all along" he said with a chuckle.

As mentioned earlier, Roy's interests were further fueled as he added two more planes, Standard J-1's, the next year. The Canadian built aircrafts were sold to the US Military. During this time the government decided they had a surplus of planes and were auctioning them off. Private owners could bid on the planes and often get them at bargain basement prices.

Roy Larson sits in the cockpit of his Curtiss Cannuck purchased in 1922.

Photo credit: Ben Joas and Theda Eckstein

"He went to Texas and bid on some Government surplus planes" Abe informed me. "He bought two planes for $125 each and had them shipped up here. It cost him $400 for shipping, more than the price he paid to acquire them." The story became more interesting as Abe continued. "That's not the best part...when he went to pick up the planes he took a team of horses and a hay wagon all the way to Neenah to collect his new additions." He explained the brothers would purchase parts and other aircraft equipment in the same bidding process from the government. "One year they bought 40 or 50 engines at a good price."

They started out in business by giving flying lessons and selling rides - $5 for ten minutes. For an extra $5 they would do some acrobatics or barrel rolls which must have been an exhilarating experience. Soon they expanded their interests and traveled around the Midwest "barnstorming" county fairs and special events. (note: The term "barnstorming" refers to individuals who travel from one area to another putting on flying exhibitions and demonstrations.) Roy even barnstormed Wisconsin for Bob LaFollette's 1924 Presidential campaign.

"Each of them flew, except Newell. He was the one who kind of stayed back and looked after things here on the farm" Theda shared. "...and Clarence was more of a promoter. He would go ahead of his brothers on barnstorming tours and sell tickets in advance for rides."

In 1926, the brothers formed the *Roy Larson Aircraft Company* where they did mechanical work and sold parts. Their dream was working. By the next year, the *Roy Larson Aircraft Company* and all their services became a new corporation titled *Wisconsin Airways*. They also acquired the rights to become the WACO agency for Wisconsin and Upper Michigan during this time.

The Larson Brothers Airport enjoyed a state wide reputation. Though modest in size and appearance, the facilities were comparable to larger metropolitan airports in spite of its rural location. Giving flying lessons was one of the many ways the Larson brothers generated income to keep the business going. Students Clyde Lee and Merle Zuehlke took flying lessons here and went on to manage airports in the Milwaukee area. Abe remembered Clyde Lee's aerial acrobatics. "One time, Lee flew his plane under the Winneconne bridge!" he said with a laugh. He added that Lee was also a first cousin of Leonard's wife, Viola. Roy Larson and Clyde Lee even partnered up on some of these barnstorming tours providing many thrills to those in attendance, some never having even seen a flying machine before. But an unfortunate tragedy would occur in 1932. (To find out more about this aviator and flying daredevil, you'll have to read on to the next chapter).

Additionally, noted aviation pioneer Elwyn West stored his airplane here and in 1928 Roy flew passengers and supplies to President Calvin Coolidge's camp on the Brule River.

Abe then reminisced about something his father-in-law Leonard shared with him years earlier. "When Paul Poberezny was seventeen years old, he contacted Leonard and said he needed an engine for a plane he was working on. Leonard said he had one and sold it to him for $5. Young Paul drove out here in his father's car and picked it up."

Leonard Larson poses next to a Waco 9 in 1927

Photo credit: Ben Joas and Theda Eckstein

When Theda talked about her father, you could sense the love, pride and admiration she held for him. "Roy being the oldest of the boys was the one my father (Leonard) looked up to" Theda said. "He always told me if it wasn't for Roy, he would never have flown." Theda has so many fond memories of her father. "When he would go on one of his 'flying times'... that's what he called it...his flying time... he would always bring us girls (four daughters) back a gift. Usually it was a can of Planters Peanuts" she said with a smile.

The date was November 25th, the week of Thanksgiving in 1929. Roy had arranged for a flying lesson with one of his students from Neenah, but as the time drew near, he decided he didn't want to go that day. "The only plane available belonged to the student and was a Swallow...one that Roy wasn't comfortable with," Theda remembers her father Leonard saying. "It didn't handle well and it was sometimes difficult to fly aerial aerobics." Theda continued "He just didn't want to go, but the student was persistent so Roy gave in." It is also said that Roy's experience with this particular aircraft was quite limited and he noted that this style of plane was difficult to get out of a tail spin.

During the training lesson with the student at the controls, the plane was intentionally put into a tailspin. Brothers Leonard and

Newell were working on the farm that day and remembered hearing and watching the plane race toward the ground. They knew by the sound of the engine the pair was in trouble. Moments later, as they watched from a distance the plane crashed killing the student immediately. Roy survived the impact but was seriously injured. Taken to Theda Clark hospital in Neenah, Roy Larson died from his injuries a few days later on November 28, Thanksgiving Day. Abe added "The plane went down near where Ridgeway Golf Course is today."

On December 14, 1929, the local Oshkosh newspaper, *The Daily Northwestern* reported the incident. The article (in excerpt) described what is believed caused the crash. The headline read:

Crash Which Took Roy Larson Robbed Wisconsin of One of Its Pioneer Aviators

On Nov. 25 of this year, while flying with a student pilot not more than five miles from the airport he established in Winnebago County when aviation was still an infant enterprise, that pilot crashed and sustained injuries which resulted in his death a few days later.

That man was Roy Larson of Larsen Wisconsin. To a career of flying that has meant more than 3,000 hours actually in the air, the climax came with the veteran aviator trying desperately and unsuccessfully to bring a plane out of a tailspin after the student operator had "froze" to the controls.

Just what transpired in the cockpit of the ill-fated biplane will never be known. That information is locked in the lips of the two occupants who are dead. It is known, however, that Roy Larson was acting in the capacity of observer, watching William Weid, the student pilot, put the plane through a series of spins and stalls, which a pilot must know in order to obtain a license.

At an altitude of about 5,000 feet, it is supposed Weid put the machine into a tailspin. The plane dropped lower and lower, and apparently did not respond to the student's frantic efforts to bring it out on a level.

It is believed that Larson took hold of the control stick in the front cockpit where he was sitting only to find that Weid was holding the stick in the rear cockpit so firmly that the controls could not be budged.

As the plane fell ground ward, apparently there was a struggle for control of the stick. Some observers, who saw the plane after it was on the ground, claim that Larson's stick was bent in the direction it should be to right the plane, but that Weid's control bent exactly opposite.

For years after Roy's untimely death, Leonard continued to work on planes, give lessons and do most of things they had always done. During World War II, airports were required to have a guard on duty 24 hours a day. If not, they had to close. "He was too old to be drafted or enlist" Theda explained. So, Leonard decided he could best serve his country by teaching pilots to fly gliders.

Leonard Larson was born in 1903, the same year as the Wright Brothers historic "First Flight". He lived until 1990 and was 87 years old when he passed away. The Larson Brothers had dedicated their life to their passion…aviation.

Grandson Ben reached over to the coffee table and finally opened the book I had seen on my arrival. My curiosity was killing me as I wondered what historic treasures it might hold. Ben opened the book and pointed to the page, showing me Leonard Larson's pilot license. "Take a look at the signature" Ben prodded me. I looked closer and under the line of 'Chairman' was the signature of Orville Wright. Both Leonard and Roy's licenses were signed by the historically famous Wright brother. For me, this put things into a totally new perspective regarding the era in which this had all taken place. The book was full of old photographs and newspaper clippings-some of which the family agreed to include in this book.

Today, if you drive to the west on County Highway II from Wisconsin Hwy 76, you will find a historical marker placed on the roadside just east of Winchester in Winnebago County. The beautiful field stone framed plaque was placed by the Larson family in 1985. In September of that year, Leonard and his wife Viola hosted a dedication ceremony with the placement of their historical marker.

The hangar can also be seen today from the road alongside the sod landing strip that is still occasionally used. In 2012, a severe storm felled one of the giant oak trees that had stood alongside the hangar since it was built. The tree fell on top of the hangar causing significant damage to the rear portion of the structure. The family did their own

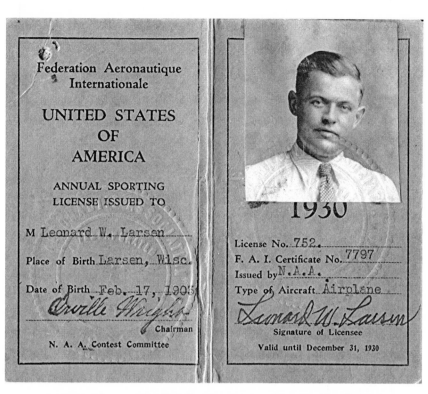

Leonard Larson's pilot license signed by Orville Wright.

Photo Credit: Ben Joas and Theda Eckstein

Larson Brothers hangar circa 2010 before a storm damaged part of the original structure.

Photo Credit: Ben Joas and Theda Eckstein

repairs and replaced things as close as they could to the original building. They also proudly point out they did this on their own accord without any financial assistance from the outside.

On October 30, 1988 Leonard was inducted in the Wisconsin Aviation Hall of Fame. Brother Roy was inducted on October 13, 2001.

The Larson Brothers Airport is listed as a historical site with the State of Wisconsin Historical Society and in 1984 was added to the National Historical Register.

(Sources: *Oshkosh Daily Northwestern*, December 14, 1929; The Wing-walker, From Wisconsin to Norway, The Larson Brothers and Clyde Lee by Bernice Lee Krippene; Personal interviews with Theda (Larson) Eckstein, Abe Eckstein, Ben Joas, 2014)

Oshkosh's Aviation Pioneer Clyde Lee

W hen I heard Clyde Lee's name mentioned for the first time, I wasn't surprised that I had not heard of him previous to working on this book. In fact, it was during my conversations with aviator Leonard Larson's daughter Theda and her husband Abe Eckstein that the history of Clyde Lee started to unfold.

Abe was sharing some family memories of Leonard Larson and mentioned that a young Clyde Lee learned to fly from the Larson brothers and one time had flown a plane under the Winneconne bridge. I found the story quite intriguing and included it in my chapter on the Larson Brothers.

About a month later, I was reading a historical overview created by the *Oshkosh Daily Northwestern* about ten years ago, and the name Clyde Lee appeared once again. So I began doing more research to see what I could find about this early aviator from Oshkosh.

As I asked around, trying to see if Lee was famous and I perhaps just had my head buried in the sand all along, I realized I was not alone. It seemed his name was not well known around town that is unless you were an aviation history buff.

The more I learned, the more I wondered why I had not heard of this man before. Clyde Lee led an incredibly exciting life. His feats were bold and required courage and great risk taking at times.

In the 1920s, aviation was still in its infancy and planes of early design were unproven in many ways. Pioneers like Charles Lindbergh, Amelia Earhart, Steve Wittman, Paul Poberezny, the Larson Brothers and Clyde Lee pushed aviation to the edge, sometimes with great risk and cost.

Clyde Lee was a first cousin to Viola Larson, Leonard Learson's wife. Like the Larson boys, Lee developed an interest in flying at an early age.

In 1923, fifteen-year-old Clyde Lee lived on a farm across the road from the Larson's near Winchester. Lee would beg Roy for a ride in that wonderful "Larson Flying Machine" and in an effort to discourage the boy Roy explained that rides cost $5. Lee stated he could come up with the money somehow and promised to return.

Return he did. In the spring after the new hangar was completed, Roy Larson taught Clyde Lee how to fly. He was now 16 and flying had become his dream. After only five lessons, Roy told Clyde he was ready to solo. As the pair had just finished a lesson, the plane was still warmed up. Clyde eagerly jumped into the cockpit, started the engine and was off. Flying over farmlands and the houses of friends and neighbors gave Clyde a thrill that soon wore thin. "What else can I do?" he immediately thought. Just then the engine started to sputter and cough. When the engine died, Clyde quickly thought to himself how thankful he was that Roy made him practice a dead stick landing. He also felt remorse that he had forgotten one of Roy's hard fast rules…always check your fuel tank before taking off.

Clyde quickly scanned the area and spotted a field that looked relatively flat and had no trees. He brought the plane down safely in the hayfield of a neighbor who was not, needless to say, pleased at the damage done to his crops. But all Clyde could think about was how pleased he was, having just completed his first solo flight. Nothing would stop him now.

As Lee worked to hone his flying skills, he was always looking for something new and exciting. He decided he wanted to learn to be a "wing walker". A "wing walker" is someone who performs an aerial stunt by standing on the wing of an airplane while in flight. Lee perfected his technique first on the ground, then once he had mastered each step, he started performing in the air.

It was about this same time in the 1920s that parachutes were invented. Of course the thrill of jumping out of an airplane appealed to young Clyde like you could not imagine. His first attempt at parachuting came in 1924 when the 16 year old accompanied the experienced flyer and stuntman, Speed Holman, to an event in Manitowoc, Wisconsin. The crowd watched in amazement as Lee climbed out on the wing and performed his wing walking feat. Holman sat at the controls, and added to the excitement by throwing in a few loops and barrel rolls. Then Lee climbed down to the lower wing and slipped on his parachute. At an altitude of 2500 feet, Lee jumped with a euphoric rush he later described as "a feeling that words cannot express". He landed safely on the hood of an automobile in the parking lot while the crowd cheered his feat.

Clyde's acrobatic feats continued, bringing fame and recognition to the young daredevil. One day, he received an invitation to meet with noted mobster Al Capone. Capone was aware of Lee's skills and wanted him to be his private pilot. Lee refused Capone's offer which paid the handsome sum of $250 a month. After hearing of Clyde's decision to decline the mobster's offer, friends were amazed and commented that "no one turns down Al Capone and lives to talk about it!"

By 1932, the young aviator's aspirations grew to epic proportions. Lee was determined to be the first American son of Norway to return to the homeland by air. An Oslo newspaper was offering a $10,000 prize to the first person to accomplish the feat of flying non-stop from North America to Norway. The amazing flights of Lindbergh in 1927 and Earhart in 1928 compelled the young flyer to make his own mark in aviation history.

Lee acquired a Stinson cabin plane to make the journey and selected fellow aviator Julius "Speed" Robertson of Negaunee, Michigan as his co-pilot and navigator.

Financing such a venture however, was not an easy task. Lee approached many local organizations around Oshkosh in an attempt to raise enough money to complete the necessary arrangements to successfully complete the Trans Atlantic flight. He named the plane "Oshkosh B' Gosh" and had the company's name painted on the side of the Stinson, hoping to lure the local clothing manufacturer to help finance the flight. His efforts here failed to raise sufficient funds when Oshkosh B' Gosh declined the offer and monies raised by local civic organizations did not meet the required levels.

The prospect of raising the needed funds seemed dismal. Then Lee heard about a group of businessmen in the Vermont communities of Barre and Montpelier who were interested in possibly financing his effort. Now Lee had the financial backing to cover the cost of rebuilding the motor in the Stinson and redesigning the fuselage by adding fuel tanks, one 100 gallon tank in the cabin and a 50 gallon tank on each wing. He also planned to have 50 five-gallon gas cans stacked inside the aircraft. This equaled 450 gallons of fuel which Lee estimated could take him 37-40 hours over the ocean. This arrangement posed quite a danger as a single spark inside the cabin could blow up the entire plane. Considering this danger, Lee decided against installing a radio on board lest a spark from it would mean the end.

The Stinson's estimated average speed was about 135 miles per hour, but with the added weight of the fuel and gear, he estimated it would only be about 95 mph. As fuel was used, the speed of the aircraft would increase. All things were considered as Lee crafted his plan, considering every possible scenario he could imagine.

The 50 five gallon tanks, when emptied would be resealed and stowed to provide additional flotation if the plane were to go down in the sea.

Clyde Lee, circa 1930
Photo Credit: Wittman Regional Airport Collection

At 12:30pm on August 5, 1932, Clyde Lee and Julius Robertson boarded the Stinson now named the *Green Mountain Boy* to promote the granite industry in his new sponsor's home state of Vermont. The plane, showing number NR7576 on the upper and lower part of the wings as well as both sides of the rudder, landed in Vermont the next day after spending the night in Erie, PA.

Harbor Grace, Newfoundland was scheduled to be the next stop before the pair would begin their non-stop flight from North America to Norway. A few days before they were scheduled to depart, Lee met a man named John Bochkon who was a former pilot from the Norwegian Navy. Bochkon told Lee he wished to accompany him on this flight and was willing to pay his passage. Still needing money, the cash-strapped Lee met with his co-pilot Robertson to discuss Bochkon's proposal. Bochkon had six years of flying experience, so he was well qualified. Robertson agreed to step back and allow Bochkon to take his place.

On August 22, Lee learned two other pilots were planning to make the same journey and the race was on. Thor Solberg and Carl Peterson planned to take off from New York at daybreak on August 23. Solberg and Peterson also planned to fly out of Harbor Grace the same day Lee was planning to leave Barre, Vermont for Harbor Grace. That would give his competitors a one day advantage.

On August 23, the Solberg/Peterson team left New York at 4:43am, destination Harbor Grace Newfoundland. They planned to stop to refuel and immediately depart for Norway.

That same day, back in Vermont, Lee and Bochkon were grounded by fog. They finally got off the ground shortly after 10am, knowing they were already behind the other team.

Both teams encountered severe weather as they raced toward Harbor Grace. The planes were pelted with rain, hail, snow and strong winds as the experienced aviators fought to make their way toward their destination. Toward evening, the airport at Harbor Grace was reporting heavy fog. Emergency lighting was put into place to assist the planes in spotting the landing strip. Anxious moments passed as ground personnel awaited their arrival. But as the evening went on, no planes arrived.

It turns out that Clyde Lee decided to put his plane down on a beach at Burgeo Bay, about 400 km short of their original destination, to wait out the storm. With no radio on board, the two were left to weather the storm providing no communication to those tracking their journey.

The next morning, Lee and Bochkon made necessary repairs to a damaged wing and softened the tires by letting a little air out from each to gain traction for takeoff.

They had little notion of the progress their competitors were making. Perhaps they made it to Harbor Grace and were already en route to Norway that morning. There was nothing they could do but continue on and hope for the best.

Coincidentally, Solberg and Peterson encountered the same weather conditions as Lee and Bochkon, but abandoned the idea of landing on Burgeo Bay beach as it was deemed to be too dangerous. Instead, the pair attempted to fly over the storm but experienced an engine stall in the process of trying to climb to 5000 feet. Before they could re-start the engine, the plane crashed into the cold waters of the North Atlantic. Solberg and Peterson both survived the crash and were rescued by fishermen. Their plane was towed to shore, too damaged to continue, so the race to Norway came to an end for this pair.

The *Green Mountain Boy* reached Harbor Grace on August 24, more than 22 hours after their departure in Vermont. Although worn out from the previous day's adventure, Lee and Bochkon refueled the plane, replaced spark plugs, checked again for damage on the wing and said "I believe that will do it." Now fully loaded with fuel and supplies, the *Green Mountain Boy* weighed 5400 pounds. In an effort to reduce weight, Lee decided to not take an inflatable raft and paddles.

Lee and Bochkon completed preparations to leave the next day. Several other groups before them had attempted such a feat and failed, many lost at sea. Would the Oshkosh aviator succeed in being the first to complete this daunting accomplishment?

On August 25, 1932, at 6:02am Harbor Grace time, Clyde Lee and John Bochkon waved to the crowd that had assembled and headed down the runway to begin the final leg of their historic journey. The heavily loaded plane lumbered down the airstrip as the engine worked hard and furious to pick up speed. Lee, unaware of his appointment with destiny, brought the engine to full speed and pulled back on the stick as the *Green Mountain Boy* slowly lifted off the ground.

From that point on, history can only speculate the details on what happened next.

The August 26 edition of the *Oshkosh Daily Northwestern* headlines read *"Lee and Bochkon Unreported In Flight To Oslo"*. Weather reports indicated calm around the Emerald Isle, but strong northwest winds were reported to be blowing 400-500 miles off Ireland's west coast. *The Northwestern* reported they were flooded by calls from concerned citizens seeking information on the Oshkosh aviator. Friends and family members in the Norwegian settlement around Winchester and Larsen anxiously waited for news and prayed for Clyde's safe arrival. *The Daily Northwestern* reported:

> As the hour for Lee's expected arrival at his destination passed at noon today, with no definite information on the planes position, scores sat at their radio waiting for news that Clyde had succeeded. The only encouraging bit of information which reached here pertaining to Lee and his companion, John Bochkon of Brooklyn, was that a red plane thought to be theirs was sighted flying over England.

Back in Oshkosh, Lee's sister, Mrs. Raymond Baxandall, sat near her radio in her home at 295 Mt. Vernon Street, feeling optimistic about her brother's success. "I feel very optimistic, and we all are very sure that Clyde will reach his goal," Mrs. Baxandall declared. "Clyde is a good flyer, and if he was seen over England he certainly will be all right," claimed a friend.

But as dawn broke the next day, there still was no sign of the courageous aviators. The August 27 edition of *The Northwestern* reported word was being sent out to steamship companies asking for their assistance in searching for a potentially downed aircraft at sea. The world waited, clinging to threads of hope that Lee and Bochkon were still alive; perhaps they landed at an alternate location due to weather or fuel issues. The anticipated time for fuel capacity had long passed, so hope and speculation circulated that Lee and Bochkon landed somewhere safely but didn't have the means to communicate their whereabouts.

By August 31, hopes had diminished and the reality began to sink in. Clyde A. Lee and John Bochton had been lost at sea. The last possible sighting was recorded days earlier by a Welsch patrol who claimed they heard an aircraft overhead and they assumed it must have been the *Green Mountain Boy.*

Their fate is unsure and left for the ages to speculate. Perhaps Lee increased his elevation to avoid bad weather. In the process they could have experienced mechanical problems or lost their direction. Did they run out of fuel? As the aircraft was never found, no one knows for certain.

In the end, the former Oshkosh High School graduate left us at the early age of 24 years old. During those 24 years, Clyde Lee lived and experienced more than most people do in a lifetime.

Author's Note: If you would like to learn more about Clyde Lee or the Larson Brothers, I highly recommend the book *Wingwalker, From Wisconsin to Norway, The Larson Brothers and Clyde Lee.* The book is written by Clyde Lee's sister Bernice Lee Krippene.

Sources: *Oshkosh Daily Northwestern*, the following dates: February 4, 1932, August 3,4,10,13,23,25,26,27,31, 1932; *WINGWALKER*, From Wisconsin to Norway, The Larson Brothers and Clyde Lee by Bernice Lee Krippene; Forward in Flight, The History of Aviation in Wisconsin by Michael J. Goc and Wisconsin Hall of Fame; www.wisconsinaviationhalloffame.org

Union Star Cheese Factory
"Purveyors of Squeaky Cheese"

I n Wisconsin, great amounts of cheese are consumed annually by cheese lovers of every age, shape and size. After all, Wisconsin is known as the dairy state, a badge of honor the locals wear proudly. At Green Bay Packer games, hundreds of fans adorn wedge-shaped foam cheese on their heads with nobility, thus giving credence for outsiders to affectionately refer to Wisconsinites as "Cheeseheads".

Located in the central region of the state, the town of Colby is known for creating the mildly delicious Colby style cheese. We have become the self-professed "Cheese Capital" of America! Travel across the state of Wisconsin and you will find the landscape dotted with dozens of local cheese factories. Some are large corporate types that manufacture cheese on a large scale while others are small, almost boutique style businesses that specialize in specific kinds of cheese. Both help support the local economy by purchasing milk from local farmers.

Winnebago County has been home to many cheese factories over the years. Historian Publius V. Lawson published a book in 1908 titled *History, Winnebago County, Wisconsin: It's Cities, Towns, Resources, People*. In it he writes, "There are more cheese factories and more cheese made in the town [ref: Town of Vinland] than any other town in the county. The town contains ten cheese factories."

One such cheese factory can be found near the northwestern corner of Winnebago County in the tiny hamlet of Zittau. A quiet little rural community with a church, a few farms and of course, a bar or two, today is the home of Union Star Cheese.

This cheese shop's connection to Oshkosh is two-fold.

The first is the owner. Oshkosh native Dave Metzig and his wife Jan have made cheese in this location since 1980. The Metzigs are descendants of a long line of dairy farmers and cheese makers who settled in this area over one hundred years ago!

Dave Metzig explains the cheese making process inside the Zittau cheese factory in 2014

Photo credit: Randy Domer

The second connection would be the popularity with local residents for "squeaky cheese". Commonly known as cheese curds, this delicious, mouth-watering morsel actually squeaks when you bite into it. Of course those of us who are most familiar with curds understand the cheese must be fresh to squeak. Once refrigerated, the squeak goes away. The flavor still remains and can be enjoyed for weeks after being processed, but they never seem to last that long in our house.

I sat down with Dave Metzig one spring afternoon in 2014 to learn about his decision to become a cheesemaker and also to find out the process used to make such delicious cheeses. It was almost 2pm when I arrived, so when Dave informed me his day starts at 4am every day, I did some quick math and realized he had been at work for ten hours already...and his day was not quite finished.

"When you own your business, you do what you have to do and work as long as it takes to get everything done," Dave said. His strong work ethic is essential to running a successful business. "I grew up in a family where my father was a veterinarian. There were no eight-hour days then either."

Dave's father, Quintin Metzig, had made the transformation from dairy farmer to veterinarian after WWII. "The war changed that generation. As soldiers returned from war to civilian life, they had to figure out where they fit in. My dad's parents ran a dairy farm near Zittau and he decided he wanted to do something else." Dave explained. "Back then, becoming a veterinarian was considered a step down from being a dairy farmer and the move was considered a big risk. Needless to say my grandparents were not real pleased." Dave then explained that the veterinarian business has evolved greatly from those times. "Back then the business mostly involved treating farm animals and occasionally some domestic pets like dogs and cats. That was before antibiotics, x-rays and all the science and technology available today."

In 1968, Dave graduated from Oshkosh High School and attended college at Valparaiso University where he earned a degree in accounting. That's where he met his wife Jan. Soon after they were married and started a family.

"I always wanted to own my own business...a small business," Dave smiled as he continued. "But as I looked at small businesses that were available, anything we could afford didn't make money and anything that made money we couldn't afford."

That's when Dave and Jan decided to look into the possibility of getting back into the family dairy business.

A photo from 1911 shows the Union Star Cheese factory in its early days. Shown standing L to R is Henry Metzig, Ida Metzig, and Millie Koenamon

Photo credit: Dave Metzig

In 1904, thirteen farmers pooled their money and built a cheese factory one block west of the four corners in Zittau. According to a recent publication titled *Town of Wolf River History, 1855-2005*, an article included within by Edna Lehman reports, " the business was called Union Star Cheese Factory because they formed a union. Adolf Hoffman was the cheese maker. After six years of running it as a union they decided to sell it to a private owner." (Edna Lehman is Henry Metzig's daughter. Henry Metzig was one of the thirteen farmers who helped organize the co-op called Union Star Cheese.) Dave explained the reason for starting the co-op came from a disagreement between dairy farmers and local cheese makers over the fat content of their milk. Milk prices were scaled based on fat content and the farmers felt they weren't getting a fair shake. So they formed their own co-op and decided to make their own cheese.

According to Dave, "Back in those days, there were more than 2,800 small cheese factories scattered across Wisconsin. When my great uncle Henry Metzig bought Union Star, he had to make a major commitment with the co-op owners, of which he was part, to close the deal…he had to agree to work on Sunday. When the business was run as a co-op, it had been closed Sundays. The local farmers' wives had been left to deal with that day's milk production themselves. This was no small task because Sundays were focused on preparing the family dinner and going to church. In the end, Henry agreed that it was better for one cheese maker to go to Hell than all the farmer's wives."

Two generations of the Metzig family are shown here as Henry Metzig works beside his daughter Edna in 1961

Photo credit: Dave Metzig

"My great uncle Henry Metzig purchased Union Star Cheese on March 1, 1911," Dave told me. Henry was the brother of Dave's grandfather,

August Metzig, who owned and operated a dairy farm nearby. Henry's daughter Edna and her husband Gene eventually took over the business. Then in 1980, Dave approached his family with the idea of possibly buying the family business. Metzig recalls, "Gene was having some health problems so he was receptive to my new interest. Edna was a little less enthusiastic as she felt we wouldn't like being in the cheese business."

Dave, wife Jan, who was an expectant mother, and their son moved into the living quarters above the factory and worked alongside Edna and Gene. In June of 1980, Dave took a dairy course at UW Madison and earned his cheese makers license. "Edna was a little reluctant at first because the process to make quality cheese was very important. She watched and worked with us every step along the way to ensure we were following the age old family process to make great cheese." In November, Edna and Gene decided to sell the business to Dave and Jan. "Edna stayed with us working for another twelve years."

Getting started wasn't easy for the new business owners. "In 1980, the cheese business was somewhat depressed." Dave recalled. "It was a time when it was difficult for small cheese factories to remain profitable. The costs of new technology meant new equipment and marketing your products was very costly." Metzig continued to emphasize his point, "In 1950 there were 25 cheese factories in Winnebago County. By 2005, only about 150 remained in the entire state of Wisconsin." Since then, the trend seems to have reversed itself, at least on a smaller level. "Today we see about two new small cheese factories each year."

When Dave took over the business, the production was mainly curds and cheddar cheese. Over the years, Dave worked to diversify his product offering and added Colby (1984), string cheese and a line of flavored cheeses. The flavored cheeses gave Union Star a niche in the marketplace. Muenster with salami, bacon, jalapenos, garlic, habanera, horseradish, hickory nuts and other scrumptious flavors are very popular with the locals and is something you cannot find everywhere.

Milk is picked up daily from local dairy farms and delivered to the cheese factory by early afternoon. "The milk is transferred to a storage tank in our facility where it is stored and prepared for the next day's production." Metzig said as he led me through the work area.

The process begins each day around 4am. "We strive for quality with no compromise," Dave assured me. "Precision is the key to making quality cheese." He pointed out the little things that can change the texture and moisture level of the finished product. "You have to be careful not to under work or over work the cheese during production."

Those delicious curds, or "squeaky cheese" that we all enjoy, are created in the process of making cheddar. "You alter a few production steps along the way and you have curds," he said.

In explaining the cheese making process to me in language I could understand, Dave talked about the costs involved in making cheese. "The yield of finished product from raw milk is about 10%. So for every 1,000 lbs of milk you start with, you end up with about 100 lbs of finished cheese."

Then there's the cost of additives such as "good bacteria" and rennet. When you factor in labor, delivery costs, overhead, etc., the margins are quite thin. "We work hard to make sure our prices are competitive in the marketplace with other products available to our clientele."

Each week, Union Star Cheese produces approximately 7,000 lbs of cheese. Metzig estimates about one third of his production is curds, one third block cheddar and one third miscellaneous cheeses. He also sells a five-year aged cheddar that is produced by another cheese maker in the state. "I'd like to age my own cheddar but it would require adding more refrigerated storage space."

In 2002 they built a second store they call "Willow Creek" near the intersection of State Highway 21 and State Highway 49, a few miles west of Omro. "The State decided to re-route State Highway 110 in another direction and the busy state highway became a less traveled County Trunk II . That decision to change the highway affected our business in Zittau by about 10-15%, so we decided we needed to add another location if we wanted to continue to grow our business."

Most of their sales today come directly from their two factory stores that offer retail products. Although they sell cheese via mail order and other retail stores in the area, two-thirds of their sales are made through their own two locations.

Today, Dave Metzig is a Wisconsin Master Cheesemaker and continues managing the business his family started over one hundred years ago. His hopes are high that one of his five sons will show interest in taking over the family business, representing the fourth generation of Metzigs in the dairy and cheese business. Sons Matt and Jon both have

The Union Star Cheese Factory Outlet Store in Zittau, Wisconsin, circa 2014

Photo Credit: Randy Domer

cheese-making licenses from UW Madison. Their journey in this craft also includes internship/apprenticeship programs which they both received at Union Star. Like any family business, the next generation of Metzigs started out at the bottom of the ladder. Jon remembers bagging curds at age five and received a penny a bag for his efforts. It is said the best way to learn any business is start at the bottom and work your way up.

So, the next time you bite into one of those delicious, squeaky cheese curds or slice off a piece of melt-in-your-mouth, hand-crafted Wisconsin Cheddar from Zittau, give thanks to people like the Metzig family and a century of hard work, craftsmanship, and tradition that make us proud to be Cheeseheads!

CLARENCE "INKY" JUNGWIRTH

There are a number of people around Oshkosh who, for one reason or another, have earned the title of "historian". They have invested a great deal of time researching Oshkosh history and have developed a deep passion for our past in Sawdust City. Looking through endless stacks of library books and working online with the internet and digital newspapers can be rewarding in uncovering long lost details of things that helped shape our city and lives. And let's face it…as we begin to age, our memories are not quite as sharp as they once were, so we have become grateful for these resources and people who enjoy researching and writing about our past.

When it comes to recalling local history, no one can hold a candle to a man we know as Clarence Jungwirth …or as his friends call him — "Inky".

Inky's passion for history is renowned in the Oshkosh area. Local folks have come to know him through talks he has given, not to mention the numerous books and articles he has written about Oshkosh's past.

I thought I was at the end of writing this book, when something happened that caused me to reconsider. I was at the Oshkosh Public Library and had just finished checking out a few books. As I was turning to leave, I heard a voice just a few feet down the counter from me that sounded familiar. I instantly recognized the voice of Clarence Jungwirth from recent telephone conversations we had this past year. I stepped back and waited for him to finish checking out before I approached and introduced myself. He clearly remembered me and we had a nice chat before parting our own ways.

On my drive home it occurred to me…"how can I write my second book on Oshkosh history without including a chapter on this man?" Previously, much has been written about him and I usually try to avoid writing about topics already covered, but this was different. It felt like my efforts would seem incomplete without including this special man.

Born in Oshkosh on October 5, 1919, Clarence Jungwirth began a journey that, when told to people today, would cause them to shake their heads in disbelief.

Inky is small in stature only, standing only five-foot-four. At 95 years old, his memory is still sharp as a tack. "God has blessed me with a wonderful memory. I can remember back to when I was four years old," he said proudly. Even more amazing is the fact he is still working today (2015). "I've been employed by Oshkosh Truck for 75 years! I tried to retire in 1987, but a few months later they called and asked me to come back!" He remembers starting work there on September 3, 1945 and today holds the title of Engineering Consultant.

I asked Inky if he would be willing to sit with me and help me write a chapter on his life in Oshkosh. He eagerly agreed and scheduled time for me to come to his office at the Oshkosh Truck Service Center located just south of town.

When the day arrived, I drove out to Inky's office and pulled into the parking lot as a light snow filtered down from the grey, winter sky. Before I could turn off the car, I looked up and there was Inky, holding the office door open and waving to me.

We greeted each other and I followed him inside as he led the way to a vacant office we would be using for the interview. "I like it in here because this office has a good heater. It's always warm in here," he said. In spite of that comment, he put on a down-filled jacket and sat down across the desk from me.

Once we started talking, it became clear to me that one could write volumes about his life. After sharing some ideas, I suggested that if there was a book to be written about his life, that book would best be written by him. He smiled with a wink and said, "Already in progress. I've been writing it for a few years now and from time to time I keep adding the most current stuff. When I'm gone it will be my autobiography. It will be my 26th book I have written over the years."

Clarence and his wife Virginia were married in 1971. "I got married late in life…later than most I guess. I was 52 years old!" he shared. "I considered myself a confirmed bachelor. That is, until I met Virginia. Virginia is the love of my life!"

We began discussing ideas on how we should approach our story. Inky paused, looked at me, and said "I think it would be a good idea to write about my military career." Clearly, it was something he was very proud of. Since much of what has been written about him previously, by himself and others, mostly covered his experiences of life in Oshkosh and local history, I agreed it would be a good idea to profile this man as few have seen him.

To provide some background, he started by talking about the early days as a young boy. "I was raised Catholic and I'm very strong about my religious beliefs even today," he said as a matter of fact. "I was baptized in Sacred Heart Church and attended school there," he stated. Then he proudly pointed out, "I graduated from Oshkosh High School in 1938 with honors."

He talked about what life was like for a kid growing up in the 1920s and 30s. "Those were some very hard times back then. Most kids never went to high school because when they were around twelve years of age, they looked for a job. It was more important to find work to help support the family than it was to attend school." I asked him why it was different for him. He replied, "well, when I was in the Army, they gave us an IQ test. I scored 148 and they considered 150 genius. I guess my mother saw something in me and insisted I continue my education by attending high school."

I asked him how he got the name "Inky". "Everyone had nicknames back then and I was a runt. They thought I was born premature, you know…an incubator baby. So they called me Inky for short."

The Jungwirth family originally lived in the Sixth Ward on Ninth Street, in what would be the 800-900 block today. Shortly after Inky was born, they moved to Sixth Street near Rugby Street.

"When I was a small child, I was blessed with a miracle," Inky told me. "I was only two years old and had wandered off and my mother could not find me. When she couldn't locate me, she panicked and ran to the neighbor's house. The neighbor lady joined in the search. No one knows why, but the neighbor went over to the rain cistern in our yard and lifted the cover. Rain cisterns were wooden tubs sunk into the ground and used to collect rainwater. Apparently I had leaned over to look inside and fell in and the cover closed on me. My overalls were caught on a nail and I was going under for the last time when she reached down and grabbed me by the hair, and pulled me to safety. I truly believe it was God's doings…a miracle."

As a teen, Inky remembers being treated differently by some of the other kids. "Back then, people with intelligence were looked down upon by some of the kids and one day I said 'to hell with them' and became a loner. There were a couple of other boys like me so we formed a clique. We were a clique within a clique."

At age 15, Inky landed a job working for a tailor, George Fisher on Washington Boulevard. "The legal age to work was 16 but that didn't stop anyone younger from finding a job," he said. Inky worked part time 6 days a week, mostly before and after school and Saturdays. "Before school I would go in and clean the shop. After school I made deliveries on my bike. I made $2 a week and that's when a dollar was a lot of money!" he exclaimed.

Clarence Jungwirth in uniform circa 1941

Photo credit: Clarence Jungwirth

Inky graduated from Oshkosh High School in 1938 and the Depression continued to take its toll making jobs scarce. He was still working for the tailor and his future looked bleak. One day in June of 1940, Inky and his pals were sitting on the porch, scheming how they could make some extra money. Someone came up with the idea to join the National Guard. "One of the fellas said they were looking for recruits," he said. So, on June 24th the boys all made their way to the local recruiting office and signed up. "They paid us $1 a week to attend drills."

As a recruit, Jungwirth was assigned to Company H, 127th Infantry, attached to the famous 32nd

Division. But there was still one hitch…he needed to pass the required physical examination before he was officially accepted. "I passed the exam with ease" Inky chirped. "It was only a general exam done by a local doctor and the general attitude of the military was… *if the body was warm - we'll take it*," he added. But that was all to change a few months later.

An old Smith-Corona "Silent Secretarial" typewriter sits poised on Inky's desk..it's heavy use, evidenced by numerous marks of correction fluid

Photo credit: Randy Domer

Inky's first job in the National Guard came early when the company clerk was relieved of his job. "I took a typing class in high school because I planned to someday be a bookkeeper and thought typing would come in handy," Inky informed me. His proficiency came quickly as Jungwirth learned there were additional benefits in being the company clerk. "No guard duty, KP, long hikes etc. that were standard fare for most other GIs." The typewriter would become Inky's constant companion…even yet today!

Originally, Jungwirth looked at his career in the National Guard simply as a way to earn some extra money to help support his family. That all changed on December 7, 1941. The Japanese attacked the United States at Pearl Harbor; an act that would draw America into conflict. The President told the country, "Yesterday, December 7, 1941—a date which will live in infamy—the United States of America was suddenly and deliberately attacked by naval and air forces of the Empire of Japan." The event was considered an act of war.

President Roosevelt announced he was activating select National Guard units, inducting them into the US Army for one year. The 32nd Division was one of them. The units had about six weeks to prepare for the induction and another physical exam would be required. Jungwirth had successfully completed many of the initial steps, but when the physical examination continued, the doctor reported that Inky had varicose veins in his right leg which would prevent him from passing the physical. Inky begged and pleaded with the doctor, trying to convince him he was fine. The physician eventually gave in and passed him.

Inky's unit was assigned to a base in Louisiana for duty preparation. During this time, Inky served as a war correspondent for the *Oshkosh Daily Northwestern*. He had his own column, titled "Handouts From 'H' Company", where Inky reported on what troops from the Oshkosh area were doing on active duty. He specifically named people and reported information on their training, duty assignments, who was on furlough, what they liked doing during their free time, etc. It gave folks back home some wonderful insights into the day-to-day routines their friends and family members were experiencing.

World War II was in full swing as Inky's unit shipped out from San Francisco on April 22 and arrived in Australia three weeks later aboard the USS Mt. Vernon. The US, which had not yet entered the European theater of the war, was fully engaged fighting the Japanese in the South Pacific. Six months later, Jungwirth and his unit were deployed to New Guinea and he saw his first real combat on Christmas Eve of that year.

In 1943, Jungwirth contracted and survived a bout of Malaria while stationed in Australia. He described his experience for me. "I had fever and sudden chills for days. They put me in the Division Hospital for ten days and I couldn't leave until the test showed negative. One of my friends was in the same hospital unit as me with a case of intestinal worms he picked up in New Guinea. Rumors were circulating that our unit was preparing to move out and we didn't want to be left behind. So my buddy and I exchanged papers when we went for our tests. I used his and the test showed no sign of worms in my stool - and he had my papers and his tests showed no sign of malaria in his blood. We were both released!" Eventually Inky ended up in a rest camp at Rockhampton, Australia where experimental drugs were used to treat Malaria. *Atabrine* (a trademark brand of quinacrine hydrochloride) was still experimental and the troops were used as "guinea pigs" to see if it worked. "They'd start us off in small doses and increased them gradually until patients started showing adverse reactions. Then they'd cut it back a bit." Inky claims the drug was effective in treating the disease.

CJ
Oro Bay
New
Gunie
1944

Clarence Jungwirth at Oro Bay, New Guinea in 1944

Photo credit: Clarence Jungwirth

Later that year, Jungwirth found himself and his unit back in New Guinea at Oro Bay . Rumors were circulating that GIs, who had served long terms in the South Pacific, were being sent home. Inky prayed he would be on that list, having served almost three years overseas and wanted to go home. On Oct 3, he was ordered to board a ship, thinking this was his trip stateside. Destinations were a closely guarded secret then for security reasons, so when the ship departed and headed north, he knew that was not in the direction he had hoped.

Jungwirth was assigned to the 24th Infantry Division as a rifleman and found himself being prepared for the invasion of the Phillipines which would take place in just a few days. Inky's heart sank. "I felt that I was never to see home again and that it would be all over for me." He felt alone being assigned to a new unit. "I was viewed as a stranger that had to prove himself all over again to each and every one of them," referring to his new comrades in arms. "It takes time to develop trust and build friendships," he added. The new unit had just completed a rough stint in combat in recent weeks and here they were making preparations for another landing. "There was no time for buddies; we were all tired of war and seeing our friends killed beside us. It was with heavy heart that I boarded that assault ship in Hollandia."

As the convoy headed out to sea, it was joined by ships from every direction. Inky recalls "There were ships from horizon to horizon. It was quite a sight with battleships, cruisers, destroyers, and submarines riding on the surface in full view. Our flanks were protected by aircraft carriers to ward off the threat of a Japanese air assault. The vessels were loaded with troops, guns, trucks, and equipment needed for a beach landing. The convoy moved at a slow pace – always no faster than its slowest vessel."

Under cover of darkness on October 19, 1944, the assault approached the Island of Leyte. Special naval forces were dispatched in advance to check for mines and potential obstacles. At 2am, the troops were awakened by the call to general quarters. As the troops quietly dressed, each man was left with his own thoughts about what might lie ahead.

As dawn broke, the naval assault began with a thunderous bombardment. Inky described what he saw that early morning. "It was a scene out of hell. Thousands of tons of shells were falling on the island. Shells from the big battleship guns came arching through the air, some looking as big as a small car." Inky's unit was to take part in the third wave to hit the beach just south of the city of Tacloban on the northeast coast of Leyte. The landing craft hit the beach with artillery fire and mortars raining around them. Most of Jungwirth's unit made it safely to shore. Inky remembers "I said my final prayers and hit the sandy beach running."

Chaos and utter confusion was the scene best described as troops stormed the beach. Hundreds of local civilians scurried around seeking safe shelter to hide from the bombardment – some carrying and waving white flags.

The mission at hand was to secure a position on high ground. Jungwirth and his unit quickly moved off the beach into rice paddies, wading through waist deep water with guns held high over their heads. At five-foot four, Jungwirth had all he could do to keep his gun dry and not step into any holes for fear he might drown. When they finally reached high ground, they discovered they had moved in the wrong direction, so back into the rice patties they waded until they reached their desired location. Once on solid ground, the officers and NCOs assembled and removed all rank from their uniforms. It was a known fact that Japanese snipers would target those with rank.

Over the next few months, the unit experienced heavy fire. Inky had become separated from his unit and tried to rejoin his company. Getting lost turned out to be another miracle in Inky's life, as during this time his company had come under heavy fire and suffered a number of casualties. He reported there were a number of incidents like this in which he escaped possible death due to unforeseen circumstances. Here is one of those examples: "The soil was very hard and gravelly and I could only dig a very shallow foxhole. That night it started to rain and my hole started to fill up with water fast. I was in a quandary. If I stayed in the hole, I could drown, if I moved out I could get shot by my own men. It was a "Cardinal Rule" that anything moving on the ground at night was an enemy target. I became desperate, so I decided to take a chance. I had a rain poncho that I pulled tightly around me and slowly moved out of my foxhole and slept on top of the ground. The next morning as we were eating breakfast, one of our men asked me if I'd moved out of my foxhole at night? I said yes and explained why. He told me he had seen something move in the darkness in my vicinity. He brought up his gun and pointed it in the direction of the moving figure and was ready to fire but somehow he could not pull the trigger. If he had, I would have got a bullet right in my head. God was with me that night…again."

The final invasion in the Philippines took place in Mindanao in April of 1945. Mindanao was one of the largest islands in the Philippines and was one of the last of the Japanese strongholds. The convoy set out from San Jose, Mindoro on April 8 with a plan to land at Parang on the east coast. Troops were told to be prepared to expect the worst. En route, news arrived that President Roosevelt had died, causing everyone to wonder what affect it would have on the outcome of the war. The movement was surprised they had not encountered any resistance whatsoever and landed without incident.

Once they had disembarked and organized, the 24th Infantry Division moved to the town of Cotabato where they were surprised to find a fleet of Navy LCIs (Landing Craft Infantry), crewed by naval personnel, ready to load them up for the assault on the Japanese. The Japanese were retreating and reports had them positioned about fifty miles upriver. The trip was rather uneventful with only a few modest encounters with Japanese rear guards along the route. Resistance increased as the troop movement closed in on the Japanese positions. Inky recalled an incident, "Panic flared one day among some GIs who, the night before, slept in a vacant hut along the river bank. The next day they discovered it had formerly been occupied by lepers. The medics had the men wash themselves thoroughly and burn all their clothing. Today, we know it is very difficult to contract Leprosy from casual contact, but that didn't help those poor fellas back then."

Inky remembered another close call that almost cost him his life. "We dug our foxhole along the road one night and I took my regular turn of staying awake and alert for an enemy attack. I had a hard time staying awake but I fought against the sleep that was trying to overtake me. The next thing I knew my buddy was shaking me to wake up. He had awakened and found me asleep. I was horrified, because that was asking for trouble. I was really shook up that morning when I learned that several of our men in a foxhole across the road had been found dead. The Japanese had sneaked up on them during the night and cut their throats. It was the first and last time I ever fell asleep on my watch."

On July16, 1945, Inky received word that his time to go home had finally arrived. He remembered praying all the way home that no unfortunate incident would prevent his safe return to Oshkosh. The Japanese had deserted the island save for a number of soldiers who fled into the shelter of caves and the thick, tropical foliage. On the water while en route to the US, concerns over being attacked by enemy submarines were foremost in their minds as the ship carrying Inky and his 2,500 fellow soon-to-be discharged comrades made the 8,000 mile trip across the Pacific without an escort. En route, Jungwirth remembers passing near the cruiser USS Indianapolis, unbeknownst to him, which delivered the components for assembling the atomic bomb on Tinian Island on July 29, 1945. One morning shortly after this, Jungwirth was shocked to hear the USS Indianapolis was sunk by a Japanese Submarine. On August 6, word was received that the US had dropped an atomic bomb on the city of Hiroshima. Three days later, on August 9, a second atomic bomb was dropped on Nagasaki and by the time their ship arrived in Seattle, Washington on August 13, it seemed the war was finally coming to an end.

Once Inky set foot on US soil, he searched until he found a phone to call home. 1,208 days had passed since he left the United States and he was homesick. "I called my parents in Oshkosh and told them I was coming home. They hadn't heard from me in a long time and were unaware I was returning." A train carried Inky from Seattle to Camp McCoy, Wisconsin where he received his final pay and discharge papers. The last leg of his trip was by train from Camp McCoy to Milwaukee, then to Oshkosh. As he rode that train on the final leg of his journey, Inky enjoyed soaking in the wonderful sights of the beautiful state he so longed to see again. As he gazed out the window of the train, his mind wandered back to the south Pacific. He thought about his best friend Andy (Andrew A. Kossl) who was killed by a Japanese sniper in the

Philippines, and he mourned his loss. He referred to Andy as "the best friend I ever had in my life - we were teenagers together." How he wished Andy would be here riding beside him today. One by one, he thought of the other friends he lost in the war and wondered why his life had been spared. He concluded that it must have been God's will that brought him home safely on this day.

As the train pulled into the railroad station in Oshkosh, anxious family members gathered to welcome home their loved ones. Waiting for Inky was his family...his father, mother, brother Bob, sister Grace and her husband Bill. His tears of sadness turned to tears of joy as he embraced each one, thankful to be back home. The date was August 27, 1945.

As our conversations came to a close, Inky helped me put things into perspective. "Of the 300 guys who left Oshkosh in 1940 to train in Louisiana, I am the only one left today," he mused softly and respect-fully.

Inky sits at his office desk at Oshkosh Corporation on December 17, 2014

Photo credit: Randy Domer

These few pages are just an abbreviated illustration, a mere snapshot of Inky Jungwirth's military service. In 1991, Inky wrote a book detailing his experiences in World War II and dedicated it to the 50th Anniversary of the attack on Pearl Harbor. The book is titled **DIARY OF A NATIONAL GUARDSMAN IN WORLD WAR II, 1940-1945** by Clarence Jungwirth. The book portrays in great detail his experiences along with newspaper articles and photos depicting actual events from the South Pacific during the war.

After reading the book, I found myself filled with respect and admiration for someone until recently, I barely new.

From this time forward, when I hear the phrase "The Greatest Generation", I will think of Clarence "Inky" Jungwirth and understand truly what that means.

Source: Personal Interviews with Clarence Jungwirth; *Diary Of A National Guardsman In World War II, 1940-1945 by Clarence Jungwirth;*

The following story is written by Clarence "Inky" Jungwirth and included here, with his expressed permission...in his own words.

WHEN I WAS EIGHT IN 1928
BY CLARENCE "INKY" JUNGWIRTH

When I was eight years old in 1928. I lived in a very poor neighborhood. My parents were very poor. My father worked at a lumber company for very low wages. Our home was three miles away from the factory where he worked from 6am to 6pm, 6 days a week.

He had to walk to and from work every day, winter and summer. My mother would pack a lunch for him to eat during the noon hour at the factory. This meant my mother and father would have to get up at 4 AM so my father could have breakfast before he started his walk to work.

There was no "Daylight Saving Time" in 1928 which meant my father had to walk to and from work in the dark. In 1928 there were no concrete sidewalks. All sidewalks were made of wood. There were many lumber mills in Oshkosh in 1928 which was the main source of work for the early males in Oshkosh.

The men had to wear heavy work shoes to protect their feet in the lumber mills. As the thousands of men walked to work on the wooden sidewalks, there would be a loud, thumping sound in the air from the thousands of feet pounding on the wooden sidewalks.

Our home was very small, consisting of only three rooms, a big kitchen, a small bedroom for my parents, a small closet where my mother would store canned goods and other items and a living room that was usually used for storing your fine furniture. This room would only be opened for parties such as at Christmas time or other special occasions.

There was no basement under our house, just a crawl space that during heavy rains would fill up with water. There were no bedrooms for myself, my brother and sister. We had to sleep on a large bed in the unheated attic of the house. In the winter time one could see the frost on the nails that held the roof shingles to the roof. We all slept on one bed as my mother and father could not afford to buy a bed for each of us. My brother and sister, who were younger than I, would sleep at the foot of the bed and I would sleep in the middle of the bed at the head of the bed.

For bed covering we had a large white bag filled with straw or feathers. It was about two feet thick and we were kept very warm, especially in the winter time, by our body heat. The attic bedrooms were unheated and there was no insulation on the walls of the bedroom. There were two windows in the attic for daylight. In the winter time, at times during a heavy snowstorm, snow would blow through tiny cracks in the window casing and in the morning we would step on the snow as we got up and went to the kitchen for breakfast.

Our house did not have electricity, water, toilet, or telephone inside the house. For light we used kerosene lamps or candles. For toilets we had to use an outhouse that was at the end of our lot at the end of a wooden sidewalk. If we had to use the toilet at night, my mother had a pail we called the "slop pail" which was kept next to the wood cooking stove in the kitchen. In that pail we had to urinate or defecate. This pail also contained the left over from cooking. Every day, early in the morning, the pail would be emptied into the "outhouse".

Our outhouse was a "two-holer". There was no toilet paper available as it was expensive to buy so we used corn cobs or newspapers or sheets from a catalogue to clean our self.

In the summer time, the smells in the outhouse were overwhelming and flies by the hundreds were also present. The door to the outhouse was on a hinge with a cutout or hole in the door for ventilation.

During the hot days in summer, the attic where we slept would get very hot and it was difficult to sleep. We would ask our parents if we could sleep on the floor in the living room which had a screen door for ventilation.

Summer time was vacation time from school and we played mostly outdoors in the school ground of the old Franklin School which was just across the street from our house. We played on the swings on the school grounds or shoot marbles or play hop-scotch with chalk markings on the sidewalk.

We had a small barn on our lot which was left over from the earlier days when you could have chickens, pigs or a cow on your property. Although the city of Oshkosh outlawed keeping farm animals by the time I was eight years old, we played in the barn which still had a hay loft.

For food, my mother would cook on a large wood-burning stove in the kitchen. The wood for the stove was kept in a wood shed attached to the rear of the house. It was there also my mother would do the clothes washing by hand using a wash board in a large tub of water. The only water available for washing clothing was water stored in a large wooden cistern placed in a hole at the rear of our house. The rain cistern would fill with water during rain storms. All homes had rain gutters on the roof of the home which fed into the rain cistern. This water was known as soft water as it had no minerals in it, thus you could make soap suds for washing. The drinking water for the house came from a hole drilled into the ground with a hand operated water pump connected to a pipe that was sunk into the ground until you reached fresh ground water that was safe for drinking.

When I was eight years old, the ground water in our neighborhood had not yet been contaminated by chemicals and other poisons as it is today and one could safely drink that water without getting sick.

It so happened that our well water was some of the best in the neighborhood and many kids would come to our water pump for a drink of water. We kept a tin cup tied to the water pump for kids and other people to use.

Families in our neighborhood had many children and we all played together making up our own games and just having fun talking and laughing. It was like a "block party" all summer long in our neighborhood. In the winter time after school and supper, we would spend all our time ice skating on the ice rinks that were made on the school grounds.

We had "snow ball fights" after a heavy snow storm, and used sleds to play with on the large mounds of snow. The wooden sidewalks were never shoveled in the winter time and the snow would pack hard on the sidewalks from the many people who walked on them.

Walking was the only way people had to get around. We walked to school in the winter time and would walk home for lunch if we lived close to school.

I attended Sacred Heart Catholic School which was only a few blocks from my house. The subjects taught at Sacred Heart School were reading, writing, religion and arithmetic.

It was Catholic School with grades from one to eight and we were taught by Nuns. Nuns were young women, who would never marry, who dedicated their lives to services of the Catholic Church such as teaching children. They dressed in black from head to foot and they maintained strict discipline in the classrooms. The average class size was about 50 children in each grade. The desks were large enough for two children.

No talking was allowed during class and if you were caught disobeying the rules, the Nuns had the right to hit you with a ruler or stick on your hands and back side. If you got a "licking" in school, you had to tell your parents and then you got another "licking" from your parents for disobeying your teacher.

Every home in my neighborhood which was made up of all Catholic families and each house had a leather strap on the kitchen cabinet which was used to discipline the children if they misbehaved in school or at home. Physical punishment of children was permitted by society and the police as long as it was not violent punishment. To disobey your parents or teacher was considered a sin by our church.

For clothing, your mother made most of your clothes except for shoes. All the mothers in the neighborhood had a sewing machine for making clothes. They could also knit socks, mittens, sweaters, make dresses for girls and make all kinds of things from cloth which was cheap to buy.

Disease was prevalent for my generation. We all got measles, chicken pox, sore throats, colds, coughs. If you got Scarlet Fever or Small Pox or Infantile Paralysis, the city authorities (Health Department) would quarantine your house with a sign, saying nobody could enter or leave the house without the approval of a Health Department official.

People in my neighborhood were very poor and could not afford to see a doctor or a dentist. You either survived your disease by home remedies or you died.

For mothers who were pregnant with a child, they only had the services of a registered nurse of which there were very few in 1928. Most children were born at home with the aid of a registered nurse. This nurse would charge a dollar for delivering a baby in your home and follow up care.

For care of your teeth you did not worry about it as you could not afford a tooth brush or toothpaste. One could clean your teeth by rubbing baking soda or salt on your teeth with your fingers. Of course many did not and consequently many kids had poor teeth, especially your early ones. One way to pull a tooth was to tie a strong string on the bad tooth, open a door and tie one end of the string to the door and then slam the door shut hard. The string would pull your bad tooth out. It was painful but it did the job for the poor people. Another way to get rid of a bad tooth was for your father to use a pair of pliers on it and work it loose until it came out.

For children of my generation it was survival of the strongest. To live a long life for my generation was a rare thing.

SMITH ICE CREAM

One of my favorite memories from my youth was the sound of the ice cream truck rolling through the neighborhood on a hot steamy summer day. The big white van was painted with the name Tastee Freeze on both sides along with illustrations of cones, ice cream bars, and assorted frozen treats. Music, rather distorted, sounding like a warped record on a kid's phonograph, emitted from the old worn out speakers mounted on top of the vehicle. We would hear the music from blocks away, which gave us time to run home and beg mom for some change to buy our favorite frozen delight. The truck would stop and kids would gather around, coming from all over like ants at a picnic. The driver then moved from the driver seat to the window on the side of the ice cream truck and began taking orders. I usually opted for a cone, although the occasional "push-up" or chocolate covered ice cream bar was good on occasion. The "push-up" was orange sherbet in a cardboard tube with a stick protruding from one end. Once the wrapper on the top was removed, you pushed up on the stick a little at a time, exposing the delicious orange treat. It should also be noted that the cones were not real ice cream, but a product called "soft serve", a frozen ice milk product. But we didn't care…it was cool, refreshing and delicious! The Tastee Freeze truck was an extension of the store's location on Wisconsin Avenue, just south of High Street where one could purchase the same items.

The 1950s was the same time the Dairy Queen chain made it's debut in the Oshkosh market. Known as a company that grows through franchising, the first store in Oshkosh opened on South Main Street in 1959. Instantly popular with adults and kids alike, the DQ brand eventually expanded to include two other locations…one on Taft Street, and the other, years later, on Murdock Ave. Through a diversity of menu choices, the DQ brand continued to grow by introducing the Dilly Bar in 1955 and the Brazier food products in 1957-58.

Some local drive-ins also carried the soft serve products, while others tried to differentiate themselves with higher quality offerings. Leon's carved out their niche with frozen custard, something that excited many locals then and still does today.

The original building at 1311 Oregon Street

Photo credit: Ethel Green

Others decided to anchor their business around real ice cream. Oshkosh had it's share of Ice Cream Parlors in the 50's. The Hergert Dairy offered homemade ice cream served over a counter in their store on Sawyer Street, while Sunlite's had two stores where you could walk in and order a cone made with real ice cream.

But one ice cream company decided to take another approach.

Smith Ice Cream was created in 1924 as an idea spawned by two men, Larry Smith and Arthur Olsen. The pair had a dream to make, package, and sell high quality ice cream. Their business model was to package ice cream to be sold by others; the idea being to ship product directly to dealers, eliminating the middle man, keeping costs in line. They setup shop at 1311 Oregon Street (old address system) in a building that formerly housed a business named Zielke and Thomas Monuments and Markers.

The partnership of Smith-Olsen Ice Cream Company was short-lived however, as the two parted ways in 1927 with Smith becoming sole owner of the business and changing the name to Smith Ice Cream. Smith soon realized if he was going to grow his business, he needed to have someone reliable and educated in the field of making ice cream. He set out to find that person.

In 1927, a young Jim Green had just graduated from the University of Wisconsin-Madison, completing a course in dairy which included making ice cream. Smith heard about Green through a mutual associate in Wausau and arranged a meeting. After a series of negations, Green and Smith shook hands. Green walked away with a contract that paid him $125 a month and Smith walked away with an educated ice cream maker. It was the beginning of a partnership that would last a lifetime.

In the fall of 2014, I sat down with Ethel Green to talk about the business she and Jim worked at their entire lives. "We were married in 1946," Ethel informed me. "That ice cream business was our life." Like any business, Smith Ice Cream had to work through some very difficult times. "On Fridays, Jim would leave the shop and travel by truck to each of the customers. Larry Smith said 'if Jim wanted to get paid, he had to go out and collect monies owed by clients,'" Ethel stated with a firm look on her face. She also related that during WWII sugar was rationed so ice cream recipes had to be altered using honey as a sweetener in place of sugar.

Larry Smith enjoys a laugh with his team of ice cream professionals.
Left to right: Larry Smith, Al Titzkowski, Andy Sitter, Wally Ostertag,
Jim Green

Photo credit: Ethel Green

Initially, the company offered five basic flavors – vanilla, strawberry, chocolate, cherry, and maple nut. In 1928, a gallon of Smith Ice Cream sold for 75¢. Through the years, Smith eventually expanded to 40 flavors. Other products produced by Smith Ice Cream included the ever popular Lunch Bar. In my days at Stangel's Super Valu, I remember filling the ice cream novelty section. Lunch Bars came in a grey cardboard carton. I would tear the top off and place the carton in the freezer case. The Lunch Bar was in a simple paper sleeve, unsealed. "What made the Lunch Bar so popular," Ethel said, "was Ambrosia chocolate and the crunchy bits in the chocolate coating." She had me guess what those crunchy bits were until I finally surrendered. She smiled and said, "It was chopped up waffle cones".

Some local drive-ins like The Hutch and Southside A&W featured Smith Ice Cream. The combination of A&W Root Beer and Smith Ice Cream made those creamy, smooth *Black Cows* so heavenly delicious.

Jim Green and Rosie Smith ride in an antique truck to celebrate the Oshkosh Centennial in 1953.

Photo credit: Ethel Green

A church picnic or Children's Day Parade could not go by without Smith's Dixie Cups. "We used canvas bags that would keep the Dixie Cups frozen for about three hours," she explained. The Dixie Cup was a small, dish-shaped carton filled with flavored ice cream...usually vanilla, strawberry, or chocolate fudge. Each Dixie Cup came with a wooden spoon wrapped in paper.

"During the depression years," Ethel recalled "Jim said the neighborhood kids would be standing around waiting for him as he returned from his delivery route. They would beg for samples and a chance to taste some free ice cream. They loved cleaning up the remnants left in the empty ice cream containers."

Larry Smith owned and ran the company until his untimely death in 1945. (See the following chapter to learn more about Smith's strange death) His business affairs were turned over to his mother and his sister Rose (Rosalia). Rose had been the company's Vice President and Secretary under Larry and assumed management of the business until her death in 1971.

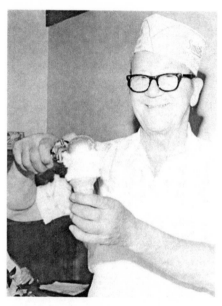

In this 1977 photo, Jim Green shows what a nickel would buy back in the 1920s

Photo credit: Ethel Green

It was then, in 1971, that Jim and Ethel decided to buy the business from the Smith family. "It was that or Jim would be out of work. He virtually ran the business for so many years, we knew what had to be done to be successful," Ethel remembered. Jim and Ethel did everything, just as you expect from a business owner. Jim handled the everyday production end of things, while Ethel handled all the administration duties.

Product quality was always paramount at Smith Ice Cream. Jim insisted the original recipe he learned from his college days at UW remained unchanged. The cream used to make the delicious ice cream was purchased from the Galloway Company located nearby in Neenah.

But time, progress, and improved technology waits for no one. In 1977, the Greens sold Smith Ice Cream to Cedar Crest Specialties, Inc of Cedarburg, Wisconsin. Ethel explained the reason for the sale. "The business growth required more production capacity and routes became too large for us to handle without making significant business changes and investments."

Coincidentally, the Kohlwey family of Cedarburg was looking to expand their business. Ken Kohlwey, current president of Cedar Crest Specialties, Inc. says, "My family started the business producing and selling caramel apples under the Cedar Crest name. That business eventually expanded into ice cream which we purchased from a company called Oak Brand." In the fall of 1976, Oak Brand closed and left the Kohlweys looking for an ice cream supplier. "We were purchasing ice cream from various ice cream makers in the state to get the flavor profiles we wanted," Ken explained.

Jim Green and new owner Ken Kohlwey worked together to ensure the quality behind Smith Ice Cream meets their standards

Photo credit: Ethel Green

That is when they heard that Jim and Ethel Green were looking to retire and their business was for sale. "Smith Ice Cream was the second largest ice cream maker in the state at the time," Ken informed me. "We approached Jim about supplying us with product and he said he wasn't sure if he wanted to do that or retire." The decision was made by the Greens to retire and they sold the company to Cedar Crest.

Production with the new company expanded capacity from their other location in Manitowoc while only select items continued to be made in the Oshkosh location. That year, production doubled to nearly 200,000 gallons of product.

The Smith brand name was used until 1982 when it was changed to the Cedar Crest brand. Jim continued to work with the new owners until his retirement in 1990. He passed away in 1997.

Ken Kohlwey estimates about 95% of the ice cream they produce today is still from the Smith Ice Cream company recipe. "The only changes we made to the original formulas were driven by suppliers. If an ingredient was no longer available, we had to make an adjustment. Otherwise most of our ice cream is from Jim Green's original recipe."

Cedar Crest continued to manufacture ice cream at the Oshkosh location until 1988. After production was relocated to Manitowoc, the store remained open for awhile, but only sold ice cream. Then, on New Year's Eve 1990, the doors of Smith Ice Cream, 1314 Oregon Street, Oshkosh Wisconsin were closed for the last time.

Today, Ethel Green still lives in the home near the former ice cream plant on Oregon Street. Her granddaughter Emily [Green] Ebel lives next door and keeps a close eye on "grandma". Emily has developed a strong interest in her family's business history and collects Smith Ice Cream memorabilia. Her kitchen wall is adorned with an old Smith calendar and assorted ice cream paraphernalia. Recently, she happened upon an old neon lighted Smith Ice Cream sign at a yard sale. She told the owner her story of her family's background in the ice cream business and asked the owner, "how much for the sign?" He reached down, picked it up and handed it to her saying "here…this means a lot more to you than it does to me". Emily is looking to have the vintage sign restored.

Source: *Oshkosh Daily Northwestern* , June 9, 1977; personal interviews with Ethel Green, Emily Ebel and Ken Kohlwey-President Cedar Crest Specialties, Inc

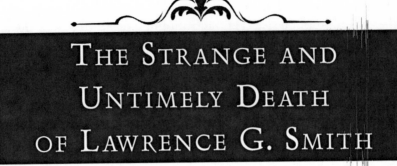

THE STRANGE AND UNTIMELY DEATH OF LAWRENCE G. SMITH

The Smith Ice Cream company enjoyed a rich and long lasting tradition as a landmark business in Oshkosh that began in 1924. President and owner, Larry Smith built the business from the ground up by manufacturing and selling high quality ice cream and frozen treats. The company gained statewide recognition based on its reputation for producing some of the best ice cream around.

Larry Smith was born in Oshkosh on June 19, 1897 and lived in Oshkosh his entire life. Along with business partner Arthur Olsen, Smith started the Smith-Olsen Ice Cream Company in Oshkosh in 1924. Two years later, Smith and Olsen went their separate ways leaving the ice cream business in the hands of Larry Smith who changed the company name to Smith Ice Cream.

Through hard work, tenacity, and strict attention to quality, Smith built a business he was proud of. But during the wee hours of the morning on Sunday, October 7, 1945, all that came to an end.

Smith was 48 years old and a widower having lost his wife in 1929. He planned to marry Mary Koelbl, his fiancée, until things went terribly wrong.

Smith and Koelbl were enjoying a night out and spent Saturday evening in and around Appleton, finishing the night at a Greenville tavern known as The Brown Jug. Around 1am Sunday morning, the couple left the tavern and headed south toward Oshkosh.

En route toward home, Koelbl complained of feeling ill, so Smith turned east off Hwy 41/45 at Erdman's Corners onto County Road G in Winnebago County just south of Neenah. According to Koelbl, Smith stopped the car about a mile east of Hwy 41/45 when she asked for a soft drink which Smith provided.

A few moments later, they noticed another car was approaching from the same direction in which they had come. When the car came along side the Smith vehicle, it paused. Smith asked the occupant of the car what he wanted and without a reply the car drove away.

Smith then proceeded to follow in the same direction the other car had headed. He had driven only a few hundred feet when Koelbl announced once again she was feeling ill and asked Smith to pull over. She then asked Smith for a cloth. With the car running and headlights burning, Smith climbed out of the car to get it for her. As he walked along the right side of the car, Koelbel said she heard what sounded like a gunshot and saw Smith fall to the ground. She called to him and Smith exclaimed he thought he was shot. Koelbl tried in vain to lift Smith into the car but was unsuccessful due to his somewhat heavy build. She reported that she looked in front of the vehicle where the headlights shown, she could see no one and assumed the shot must have come from the rear.

Gripped with fear, Koelbl decided to drive east, away from what she thought was the direction of the shot, to County Road A, leaving Smith lying on the ground. After trying unsuccessfully to flag down another motorist, she drove south into Oshkosh to the city police station and reported the shooting to authorities.

County Sherriff officers were immediately dispatched to the scene. Officers Eugene Meigher, Victor Jordan, and Harry Krippner were the first to arrive and reported Smith apparently was dead. The time of death was listed at 1:40am. Smith's body was transported to Theda Clark Hospital in Neenah where county coroner Dr. G. A. Steele said Smith had died a brief period after he had been shot.

With the shooter still at large, Sheriff Clarence Smith organized an armed posse to search the surrounding area for the suspect.

Armed with information from interviews conducted in the area the next day, an arrest warrant was issued by Winnebago County District Attorney Rudyard T. Keefe for one Herbert Erdman.

Information gathered by investigators led them to believe that Smith may have been a victim of mistaken identity, and the search for

Erdman became intense. By the end of day Monday, Erdman was still at large and authorities were quickly gathering critical evidence that pointed to him as the key suspect.

Key facts started to emerge as authorities learned of Erdman's troubled past. He had openly expressed his love for his second cousin, Jane Erdman, but his attempts were rebuked by her as he had a reputation locally as a heavy drinker. Herbert had previously warned and threatened Jane's suitor to "stay away from her". It was believed Smith's car was similar to that of Jane's boyfriend's.

The search for Erdman continued and Tuesday morning fresh foot prints were discovered by a gate near the spot where Smith had first parked and several hundred feet to the rear of the shooting. Farmers in the area reported hearing a gunshot that morning around 7:40am. With this new information, deputies doubled the search and sent the posse over the grounds again.

Shortly after 1:30pm on Tuesday, the body of Herbert Erdman was found at the bottom of an embankment in an abandoned shallow gravel quarry on his father Gus Erdman's farm. The coroner ruled Erdman had been dead about six to eight hours which coincided with earlier reports of a gunshot heard. Three partially empty bottles of liquor were found on his person.

Ballistics showed the bullet that killed Smith was from a .30-.30 cartridge, the same as found near Erdman's body. The gun found with Erdman was a .32 special Marlin rifle, old and loaded with seven shells. One empty casing still remained in the chamber, the one Erdman used to kill himself. A search of Erdman's clothing found a "badly written note" in an inside trouser pocket where he had scrawled he was "madly in love with" Jane and could not live without her. It was signed "Herbie".

As authorities worked to piece things together, they were able to determine that on Wednesday of the previous week, Erdman learned that the girl he was in love with was to go to a dance at the Valley Garden on Saturday night. Erdman's steps prior to the murder were traced and it was discovered that he had visited a bar in Butte des Morts the previous Friday night and offered a motorist there $5 to take him to a tavern near Erdman's Corners. As they left the tavern and walked to the car, Erdman ran across the street in Butte des Morts and picked up a rifle he had left leaning against a building. When they reached the tavern at Erdman's Corners, Erdman offered the driver another dollar to take him to Gillingham's Corners, a few miles north. That is where the driver left him. Later, it was discovered the rifle was stolen from Ervin Erdman's cottage in Butte des Morts and the bullets were taken from the home and store of Herbert Porath at Gillingham's Corners where earlier in the week Porath had refused to sell the ammunition to Erdman.

Erdman's jealousy was well known in the area. After making threats at Jane Erdman's father's home, Norman Erdman had constructed an electric warning device out of fear of his cousin. The device proved worthy as it was tripped Monday night while Erdman was on the run from authorities. Norman fired several gunshots into the air to ward off the intruder, figuring it was Herbert who tripped the device. Norman then alerted authorities.

The last report of anyone seeing Herbert Erdman was early Sunday morning on October 7th when he left Vi and Joe's Tavern at Erdman's Corners. It was reported he left shortly before 1am. Witnesses reported seeing a man fitting his description staggering in what appeared to be a drunken stupor along Hwy 41/45. Known by locals to have recently been sleeping in the local woods, authorities extended their search to include woods and fields. There they found evidence that someone had been lying in the grass on a slightly raised mound only about 100 feet from the scene of the murder and within view of the farmhouse in which the woman he loved had lived. Footprints found there matched the boots that Erdman was wearing when his body was discovered. It was speculated that he may have been lying in wait to ambush Jane Erdman and her suitor.

Funeral services for Lawrence G. Smith were held on Wednesday, October 10, 1945 at Fiss & Bills Funeral Home and St. John's Catholic Church. Smith was buried in Oshkosh's Riverside Cemetery.

Source: *Oshkosh Daily Northwestern*, October 8, 9, 10, 18, 1945; Coroners Report, October 1945, Barry Busby, Coroner 2015

THE STORY OF PATRICK FLANIGAN "YOU'LL SHOOT YOUR EYE OUT, KID!"

I'm a huge fan of the holiday classic film "*The Christmas Story*". In the movie, the lead character is a nine year old boy named Ralphie. More than anything, Ralphie wants a genuine Red Ryder 200-shot Carbine Action Air Rifle for Christmas. Through much of the movie, Ralphie plots ways to convince his parents he's old enough and begins his campaign by asking Santa and dropping hints to his parents. His efforts appear to be in vain when his mother tells him it is not a good idea because "You'll shoot your eye out". He also gets the same response from Santa causing Ralphie to think he would never get the ultimate Christmas present. In the end, Ralphie does get the air rifle for Christmas and all ends well. Ironically, I seem to recall having similar conversations with my mom who also feared the worst. I, too, did get a Daisy Air Rifle for Christmas one year.

Such was not the case with a young Oshkosh boy named Patrick Flanigan.

Oshkosh native Patrick Flanigan was raised in a family who enjoyed hunting. His father, Mike and uncle "Zeke" were avid hunters and taught Patrick and his brothers, at a very young age, how to respect and properly handle a firearm while embracing good hunting ethics. Little did anyone expect this young shooting enthusiast would one day become a world champion shooting expert.

I caught up with Patrick one Sunday afternoon in February of 2015. He had heard from his dad that I wanted to write his story, and he was eager to tell me how he got started in the sport of extreme shooting.

The rural area that surrounds Oshkosh is full of fertile farm fields, lakes filled with marshes, and lush woodlands that provide the perfect setting for a young boy to learn how to hunt. Young Patrick took advantage of every opportunity to hunt with his dad, uncle and brothers. "My uncle "Zeke" (Frank Paulus) was my hunting partner and mentor. In our family, hunting was truly a family event," Patrick shared with me.

Patrick's father, Mike, is credited with instilling strong hunting ethics and gun safety with his boys. Patrick and his brothers began hunting with their dad by walking behind, carrying unloaded guns. This method taught the boys gun safety and how to aim and squeeze the trigger when a shot opportunity presented itself. "The urge to hunt hit me at quite a young age," Patrick said. "I remember having this plastic toy gun that fired orange plastic pellets. I made a rabbit by stuffing an old shirt and drawing a rabbit face on it to use for practice. I would set the rabbit up at the end of the hall, lie down in a reclined shooting position, and take shots at the fake bunny," he said with a chuckle. "Sometimes those orange pellets only went a couple of feet so it wasn't dangerous or anything." This went on for several years until Patrick was finally ready to hunt with a loaded gun. Many hours were spent in the field, without a gun in hand, as his dad explained what to do and what not to do when hunting wild game. Good hunting ethics and gun safety were key to enjoying a successful hunt. It turned out to be a very effective method of learning to hunt, and years later, Patrick would apply the same method in teaching his children to hunt.

At age 14, he tried his hand at shooting clay targets. His best childhood friend and his friend's father introduced Patrick to clay shooting by starting out with hand throwing single targets. Soon they advanced to shooting at the range where the clay targets were numerous and moved much faster. Shooting clays came easy and natural to young Patrick and soon he was shooting in organized tournaments.

At about age 19, Patrick began to learn about exhibition shooting by watching videos of legendary shooter Herb Parsons who performed

Patrick Flanigan

Photo Courtesy of patrickflanigan.com

in the 1950s. Thrilled by what he saw, Patrick started trying to imitate the shots Parson made famous. What started as a casual interest soon blossomed into something more.

In college, Patrick attended a business marketing class where his assignment was to "turn yourself into a product and sell that product". As Patrick was also the youth minister at his local church, he consulted with a pastor friend of his about the assignment. His friend suggested the idea of "doing what you are best at, and what you might become." His first inclination was to expand his interests as a professional drummer. "I was an entertainer at heart, long before I became interested with shooting," Patrick told me. As early as age 13, he played drums for a few local bands including the Sundance Show Band. His interest and drumming skills earned him the chance to play professionally with Country Music star Aaron Tippin. That idea was quickly discarded when his friend reminded him of his other interest...hunting. He suggested Patrick consider filming his own TV show which would be the "product" the assignment required.

Flanigan liked the idea and began producing a show he called "Midwest Wings". "I wanted to do a hunting show that was filmed in a more natural environment on public hunting lands, not on a closed, private, high fenced property like many of the other shows were doing," he said. The show was soon picked up by the Sportsmen's Channel and Patrick was well on his way. The program provided a format that would lead the Oshkosh native into the world of extreme shooting. "We had a weekly feature on the program we called 'The Shot of the Week'. I would demonstrate a different trick shot each week." The segment was well received by viewers and Patrick knew it was something he wanted to do more of. He successfully passed the college course and kept the TV program going. Unfortunately, the show wasn't producing much in the way of income.

Flanigan decided to continue his career path as an outdoor show producer and set out in pursuit of sponsors. His first attempt was to approach the Winchester company that made the guns that he enjoyed using and were most familiar to him. At first the repeating arms company turned him down saying his shooting was good but his TV show was terrible. They suggested Flanigan look into exhibition shooter Tom Knapp's efforts with Bernelli. Knapp was a well established and experienced exhibition shooter for about 25 years. When Winchester executives asked if he could put together a show like Knapp's for Winchester, Flanigan quickly replied that he could. His reply came spontaneously and without thought, but he was confident he would figure out how to do it. Patrick traveled to Knapp's shows to observe his technique and worked to develop his own style of extreme shooting. Knowing he wanted to attract a younger audience in addition to fellow shooters and hunters, he added music and fireworks to expand the entertainment value of his show.

In his shows, Patrick's exhibitions include various types of firearms such as shotguns, rifles, and pistols. Today, (as of this writing), Patrick Flanigan is the holder of nine world records. He is listed as the *fastest shotgun shooter in the world*, his 9th and most recent title, was claimed by firing 12 rounds in 1.297 seconds, breaking his own previous world record time of 1.42 seconds.

Here is a list of the world records held by Patrick as of March 2015:

Xtreme Record #1 - Five clay targets hand thrown, individually shot, from the hip and without assistance. May 5th 2005.

Xtreme Record #2 - Eleven clay targets hand thrown, individually shot, from the shoulder and without assistance. July 6th 2005.

Xtreme Record #3 - Eight clay targets hand thrown, individually shot, from the hip and without assistance. May 16th 2006.

Xtreme Record #4 - Nine clay targets hand thrown, individually shot, from the hip and without assistance. July 6th 2006.

Xtreme Record #5 - Six clay targets hand thrown, individually shot with a pump shotgun, from the hip and without assistance. August 2006.

Xtreme Record #6 - 12 rounds shot in 1.42 seconds with the Winchester SX3 on April 3rd 2007.

Xtreme Record #7 - Seven clay targets hand thrown, individually shot, from the hip, with ONE hand and without assistance. April 2010.

Xtreme Record #8 - Seven hand thrown clay targets, individually shot, from the hip, without assistance and with a Mossberg 500 PUMP shotgun.

Extreme shooting, by definition, means taking the normal act of shooting a firearm to the extreme. In his exhibition as an Xtreme Sports shooter, Flanigan demonstrates his skills by tossing three paint balls into the air and using a .22 rifle, and bursts all three balls before they hit the ground. Then he takes three aspirins, again tossing them into the air, and breaks all three with one shot apiece. Long distance shooting is another demonstration that Flanigan uses to thrill and amaze his audience. Placing an aspirin on a board at 200 yards, he successfully hits it using his .22 rifle. He says he likes to use the .22 rifle in his show as many of the young hunters and shooters often start out with that firearm.

One day as Flanigan was filming his TV show called "Shell Shocked" for the Sportsmen's Channel, he was asked to compete against other professional shooters. The show's producer arranged for Patrick to compete against a cowboy action shooter. Not being familiar with that type of action shooting, Flanigan had to quickly learn and become agile on a whole new angle of shooting…and he only had 24 hours to do it. He spent the entire day practicing to draw his revolver, shoot, and hit a target. He whittled his time to draw, cock the hammer, aim, and break a target down to .6 seconds. Patrick continued to work with his "cowboy" partner and soon was able to throw out multiple targets and hit them with a .45 caliber revolver. Soon he was able to throw one or two targets in the air, draw, fire, and re-holster the revolver in less than a second. We talked about this feat and Patrick shared a little secret with me. "Actually, I ended up beating the pro that day on the show, but the producers didn't like the idea of me showing up the shooter as it might appear to the viewers that it may have been staged. We did it to preserve the integrity of the show."

Flanigan continues to strive to improve even though his accomplishments are the best in the world. Many of the records he owns are the result of breaking his own previous marks. Like anything else, discipline and practice seem to be key to his success. In a 2010 article from the newspaper, the *Black Hills Pioneer*, his practice to attempt another world record was described as "…he started shooting at 10am Tuesday with 15 boxes of clay pigeons. Each box contains 135 targets. When he took a 10 minute break to squeeze in an interview at around 2pm, he was down to three boxes."

Patrick performs dozens of live exhibitions each year and has a heavy schedule with over 60 events planned on his "Spray and Pray Tour 2015". He has starred in many programs in recent years including programs such as "Hot Shots" on NBC Sports, "Impossible Shots" on the Outdoor Channel, and of course his own program "Shell Shocked" on the Sportsmen's Channel. He has been featured in hundreds of publications including Outdoor Life, NRS's In-Sights, Pheasants Forever, and Ducks Unlimited only to name a few. Over the past few seasons, Patrick has taken a hiatus from the TV sports show circuit but is working on a new deal with a major network – something he is not ready yet to reveal.

Being a celebrity in Extreme Shooting puts Patrick in a whole new league of company. He's rubbed shoulders with Ted Nugent, hunted with MLB Legend Will Clark, and shouldered a shotgun with Matt Hughes, the 9-Time UFC Welterweight Champion. His rolodex contains other star athletes like Eli Manning and much of the NFL's New York Giants football team.

Patrick uses his talents to help others and the communities in which he lives in many ways. He is proud to be a strong and devoted Christian and works to create youth programs to educate and promote gun safety. He has started the "Take 'Em Out" Foundation to raise funds to help develop firearm safety, awareness and knowledge to America's youths and adults. He teaches firearm safety courses free of charge.

In his free time, which he tries to schedule during the fall hunting season, Patrick enjoys all types of hunting but prefers "wing shooting". Today Patrick, his wife Jenna, and their three children make their home in Sturgis, South Dakota. He purchased land in the Black Hills in South Dakota and returns home to Wisconsin to visit family and hunt with his dad and brothers each fall. "When I started in this business, people warned me that if you're doing this because you love hunting, you'll never find time to go hunting! They were right. I make sure I schedule my free time to hunt with my kids and family back home in Oshkosh. Duck hunting is still one of his favorite sports. I asked him where he hunts when he comes home and he said, "I ask my dad where he wants to go. He decides because, well, that's the way it always was growing up…and he's still my dad." They have their favorite places where they've always gone. "That's why I come home."

You can watch Patrick Flanigan's shooting expertise by visiting his website, www.patrickflanigan.com or just type his name into the search bar on YouTube.

Patrick and his daughter, Brinna, share some daddy/daughter time. Hunting is a long standing tradition in the Flanigan family.

Photo courtesy: patrickflanigan.com

Sources: www.mossyoak.com/our-obsession/blogs/prostaff/2014/07/ 07/a-gun-show-not-to-be-missed; www.bhpioneer.com/local_news/article; www.patrickflanigan.com

CHIEF OSHKOSH

O ne cannot begin to explain the history of Oshkosh without delving into the origination of its namesake.

Long before it became a city, Oshkosh was prairieland, located in the heart of wilderness surrounded by numerous lakes and rivers, making it the ideal habitat of Native Americans.

The Menominee tribal lands included the area we now know as Oshkosh. Its leader was Os-cosh, O'skash, or Oiscoss (many different spellings of his original name can be found in historical records), a Menominee name meaning "brave" or "The Claw". Community founders selected the name from a short list of others which included Athens, Fairview, Oceola, and Standford. The name of the popular chief was chosen and for unknown reasons, the letters were rearranged making the name Oshkosh.

Chief Oshkosh was born in 1795 on the west bank of the Fox River at the Chakauchokama's (The Old King's) Village near Green Bay. He was married three times and had three sons and a daughter. A warrior from the age of seventeen, Oshkosh gained notoriety fighting for the British in the War of 1812. He was involved with the capture of Ft. Mackinaw in 1813 and fought in the battle in Ohio at Ft. Sandusky. At the treaty meeting at Little Butte des Morts in August of 1827, Oshkosh was named Chief of the Menominees by the US Government.

Over the years as Chief, Oshkosh worked to create good relationships between the European white settlers and the local Natives. It is said he never raised a tomahawk to a white man. But in 1870, the revered chief was charged with murder.

According to a document held in the archives of the Wisconsin Historical Society, Oshkosh exacted revenge according to the Indian

"Law of Retaliation"… "an eye of an eye, a tooth for a tooth". In a manuscript dated February 1870 penned by Henry S. Baird, he writes…

On one evening in the month of May, a young half breed/part Indian and part white, started in his canoe for a torch light hunt. [Authors note: Okewa was the name of the individual referred to as a 'half-breed', a member of the Pawnee tribe] *He ascended East River three or four miles above the present City of Green Bay, and when slowly gliding along the stream, He heard a slight noise in the bushes on the bank: the night was dark; his torch shed a little light in advance of the canoe. Supposing the noise to be caused by deer feeding on the edge of the stream, he cautiously approached until he could discern an object within gunshot, and believing it to be a deer fired his gun, heavily loaded with buckshot: he saw the object drop and immediately approached the spot, when instead of a dead deer, to his horror he found the body of a dead Indian! The Indian had been sitting in his canoe without a torch when seen by the hunter, probably watching a deer salt lick. The man killed was a young Indian, a nephew of Oshkosh, one of the principal chiefs of the Menominee Nation. This Chief with his family including the young man killed had arrived at Green Bay, a day or two previously and erected his lodge on the west bank of the Fox River… The unfortunate half breed finding the Indian dead, and recognizing him as the relation of Oshkosh, abandoned his canoe and embarked in that of the Indian with the dead body and started for the lodge of the chief: arriving there about daylight, he fastened the canoe and went to the lodge and found the family yet asleep. He immediately communicated to Oshkosh the sad intelligence of the death of his nephew and explained how it had happened. The chief arose and without making any reply, followed the half breed to the canoe where the corpse was — having previously armed himself with a knife, such as Indians usually carried. Arriving there the half breed entered the canoe and walked toward the stern where the body lay, intending as was supposed to assist in carrying it to the lodge. The chief did not enter the canoe but waded alongside the water…until he came alongside the half breed, when he suddenly turned and stuck him with the knife several deadly blows: the half breed fell dead instantly.*

Chief Oshkosh was arrested, jailed, and arraigned to face murder charges in the court of Judge Doty. The jury found that Oshkosh was Indian "in habit, character, and education and wholly uncivilized." They also recognized that Native Americans lived within their tradition and obeyed the laws of their nation, and therefore recommended to Judge Doty that the accused should be held accountable by those same laws and traditions. During his consideration of imposing judgment and sentencing, Doty affirmed that Indians were not part of the population to whom political power was given and civil rights granted. He also recognized it had not been the understanding within the community that Indians possessed all the rights and privileges of civilized man.

Chief Oshkosh was exonerated of his accused crimes and released from custody, an act that would strengthen Indian faith in the justice system of the white man.

In August of 1858, at age 63, Chief Oshkosh died after a brief illness (some say caused by troubles between himself and his son). His son was an Indian agent at the time and was pressuring his father to sign over land rights to the US Government. It was said the tensions of this act grieved him so much that death soon followed. One day a fight broke out between Oshkosh and his son or sons depending on which story you believe. It is alleged that it was injuries from that incident that brought on his demise. Other accounts say the Chief was a heavy drinker, and fell victim to the bottle...a trait which was also passed along to his sons.

The body of the deposed Chief was laid to rest on the Menominee Reservation at Keshena near Shawano. Oshkosh "requested his tribe, when he died, to bury him in a sitting posture, with his pipe, tobacco pouch, gun and powder horn and pouch, one beaver trap and a rat trap, so that he might be properly equipped when he arrived in the good hunting ground."[3]

On May 25, 1926 the city of Oshkosh celebrated Chief Oshkosh Day. Through the efforts of a few Oshkosh dignitaries, arrangements were made to disinter the body of Chief Oshkosh and move him to a place of dignity and respect within the city named after its famous Native leader.

Costs for the removal of his remains to the new resting place in Oshkosh were funded through the generosity of Alfred C. McComb, the son of an early settler in Wisconsin. McComb, it is said, claimed "the experience proved to be very educational and felt well repaid for his expenditure of some twelve thousand dollars, to put on the observance …"2

A monument was placed in Menominee Park overlooking the shores of beautiful Lake Winnebago. Following a parade the remains of Oshkosh were laid to rest amid the beating of tom-toms of Native American chiefs. The monument, marking the new burial location of the old chief, was placed by Colonel John Hicks of Oshkosh. Participants in the celebration included Ernest and Reginald Oshkosh, grandsons of the great chief, and granddaughter Princess Alice Oshkosh was the keynote speaker for the dedication. A large number of Indians from the reservation in Keshena, Wisconsin attended the ceremony to pay tribute to their great leader.

Not long after this, trouble started to brew as questions were raised whether or not it was the body of the great chief that now lies at rest at the foot of the Chief Oshkosh monument. *The Milwaukee Journal* published an article on August 1, 1926. Its headline read "Chief Oshkosh Not Buried in Oshkosh, Indians Claim". A Shawano man named S. F. Luckenbach claimed to have proof the body that was moved from the reservation to Oshkosh was nothing more than a hoax. Luckenbach was a 35 year resident of the Shawano community and had forged many relationships with the local natives. On a recent fishing trip with some of his Indian friends, comments regarding the movement of Chief Oshkosh came into conversation. "Really too bad they moved the body of Chief Oshkosh away from the reservation" Luckenbach commented. The comment was met with the reply "They didn't." Luckenbach was directed to speak with John Wapoose, a 100 year old Native American. Wapoose and Luckenbach walked to the Chief's grave with Wapoose insisting the chief still lies in his original grave. He pointed out that the body moved to Oshkosh for reburial, had buttons on the clothing like that of an old woman, possibly one of the chief's wives.

In an interview as recent as 1998, Gary F. Ehlman, Communications Director for the Stockbridge-Muncie Tribe, revealed that Chief Reginald had played a trick on the city. This has also been confirmed by David J. Grignon, Menominee Tribal Historic Preservation Officer, that it has been common belief (not necessarily based on fact) since 1926 that the body moved to Menominee Park was not the body of Chief Oshkosh.

It is believed that several funerary items gathered at the time of the disinterment were once held by the Oshkosh Public Museum. The museum has recently confirmed the items eventually were returned to the tribe. Refutable evidence has yet to be presented to validate or discredit the remains to be that of Chief Oshkosh. For now, the story remains part of local legend.

Source: (1) Wisconsin Historical Society; (2) Oshkosh One Hundred Years a City 1853-1953, Clinton F. Karstaedt Editor; (3) www.rootsweb.ancestry.com/; (4) Oshkosh Public Museum PastPerfect-online.com; (5) http://www.accessgenealogy.com/native/biography-of-chief-oshkosh.htm;

JIM VANDEHEI

I f you are an early morning person like I am, you may occasionally watch some of the national news programs that, along with a cup of freshly brewed coffee help start the day. One of my early morning favorites is MSNBC's *Morning Joe,* one of the few news programs that works to provide nonpartisan coverage of the nation's political front. The cast of the program has been carefully assembled to provide diverse and opposing viewpoints to the day's issues.

Jim VandeHei, CEO and President of Politico

Photo credit: Courtesy of Politico

If you are a regular viewer of the program, you will know that one of the regular guests on *Morning Joe* is a political analyst named Jim VandeHei, CEO and President of Politico, a nonpartisan media company that covers national politics and Washington governance. What some people don't realize is that Jim is an Oshkosh native with strong local loyalties to his upbringing. Living in and around the nation's capital has not wavered VandeHei's allegiance to the Green Bay Packers and continuously reminds the public that he is a "midwestern boy" from small-town Oshkosh.

The middle child of John and Joan VandeHei, Jim grew up on the southside of Oshkosh in the Huntington Downs neighborhood, near 9th Avenue and Highway 41. John and his wife Joan are retired and still live in the rural Oshkosh area. John agreed to meet with me to talk about his son's meteoric career.

Born here in 1971, Jim attended parochial school throughout the early years of his education. Sacred Heart, a south side catholic church and school located in Oshkosh's "Hi-Holder" district, is where Jim attended elementary and middle school. He graduated from Lourdes High School in 1989 and attended college at the University of Wisconsin-Oshkosh, graduating in 1994 earning a degree in journalism and political science.

John shared some background on his son's early years. "Jim was not the best student as a kid. He was more interested in sports than academics." He pointed out that Jim enjoyed statistics. "The first thing he did when he came home from school was to grab the sports page. He followed all the local professional teams, but baseball and football were his favorites. He could tell you each of the Milwaukee Brewer's batting average and could cite facts on his favorite Green Bay Packer player."

John continued to say that Jim's guidance counselor at Lourdes High School suggested to Jim in his senior year that he either join the army or get a job working in a service station. "His grades really didn't support a higher career goal in the eyes of his counselor." John was outraged with the counselor's assessment, and told Jim very clearly that he could do whatever he put his mind to. That memory, lesson, and fatherly support still remains fresh with Jim today.

According to his dad, Jim's persona was always one where he would stand firmly on principle, no matter what the topic was. "He would seek out what he felt was reasonable and fair whether it was a professional sports contract or his own personal situation at home." John went on to explain, "I'll give you an example. Jim's brother John wore glasses and braces on his teeth and his sister Julie wore glasses and was going to need braces. Jim approached us with the idea that because he had perfect eyesight and straight teeth, he was entitled to the cash equivalent that his parents saved in not having to provide these things to him." I asked John if Jim was successful with this early negotiation. He replied with a grin "No way!"

As Jim was preparing for college, his passive approach to study started to impact his thinking on what he wanted to become. His grades weren't high enough to get into college and that's when he realized, if he wanted to achieve his goals in life, it was time to get serious about his education. He attended the UW Fox Valley extension in Menasha and worked hard to bring his grade point average up. Soon

Jim was enrolled in Journalism and Political Science courses at UW-Oshkosh, two areas he had a strong interest in.

During his early years at UWO, Jim arranged to work part time at the *Oshkosh Daily Northwestern*, landing a job on the sports desk. As a brand new "cub reporter" Jim spent much of his time covering the local sports teams. The opportunity gave VandeHei a "taste" of what a career in journalism might be like. In 1993, he took a summer job at the *Brillion News*, a small town newspaper that was published once a week. This newspaper was pretty much a one-man operation featuring stories like "Police Receive Report of Dog Barking", but it gave Jim more experience and exposed him to another dimension of media publication. The publisher at the *Brillion News*, Zane Zander, told Jim when he accepted the job that he would need to run the newspaper the entire summer. VandeHei explained he had no experience, but Zander was willing to take the risk anyway. Jim claims he learned more in two months at *Brillion News* than in the totality of journalism classes.

As he entered his senior year of college at UWO, VandeHei was approached by his journalism professor who helped him land a job working in Senator Kohl's office. Some say the best way to learn anything is to start at the bottom and work your way up. Answering phone calls from constituents was about as close to the bottom as you can get, but it gave Jim valuable insights into the political arena that one day would pay big dividends. That job, with the Wisconsin Senator, lit a fire within him and the vibrancy of that experience motivated Jim to become more interested in Washington politics.

In 1994, VandeHei graduated from UWO and a year later moved to Washington DC to pursue a career in political journalism. His first job was to report on the alternative fuels industry for the *New Fuels Report*, a weekly newsletter. Then, in 1996, Jim started writing for *Inside the New Congress*, a now-defunct weekly newsletter that covered the House and Senate.

His next assignment was as congressional correspondent for Roll Call. There he covered the fall of House Speaker Newt Gingrich and the subsequent battle for power within the Republican majority. Jim was one of the first journalists to report on Republican efforts to explore impeachment of President Bill Clinton and the withdrawal of Representative Bob Livingston's interest to become Speaker due to an extramarital affair.

VandeHei had begun to make a name for himself inside the beltway, and in 1999 *The Wall Street Journal* recruited him to cover Capitol Hill. One year later *The WSJ* named him White House correspondent which covered the first year of George W. Bush's administration.

The Washington Post tapped Jim in 2002 and offered him a position covering Congress, which led to him covering the Democrat's posturing for the nomination in 2004. With *The Washington Post*, VandeHei also served as one of the White House correspondents during the early part of President George W. Bush's second term.

But a reporter wouldn't be a reporter if he didn't ruffle a few feathers along the way. In her book titled *Spoken from the Heart*, former First Lady Laura Bush recalls a time when VandeHei may have stepped over the line during a visit to Egypt. Mrs. Bush writes:

> *After the television taping, Suzanne Mubarak hosted a lunch in my honor and then we toured Abu Sir, one of Egypt's thousand "girl-friendly schools," dedicated to girls and built in 2003 in the shadow of the pyramids. From there we saw the pyramids themselves. With the press in tow, I was in the middle of a tour with Dr. Zahi Hawass, who directs the Giza pyramids excavation. He was preparing to unveil a new discovery when Jim VandeHei, then a political reporter for The Washington Post, elbowed his way to the front of the press pool, climbed onto the pyramid plateau and began shouting out questions about the Egyptian referendum and Hosni Mubarrak's political and election plans. Dr. Hawass appeared dismayed and completely taken aback to have this outburst happen in the middle of Egypt's premier historical site. It was a violation of protocol, and as far as the Egyptian antiquity experts were concerned, Jim VandeHei was part of the U.S. delegation. Sometimes members of the press forget that they are not seen as independent entities abroad. I quietly apologized, knowing that this incident would not be attributed to an individual reporter or The Washington Post; it would be blamed on me and, by extension, on George.*

Jim recalls Laura Bush being very candid about her anger. Her staff "froze him out" and the First Lady cancelled an interview with him. Compelled to offer some clarification to Mrs. Bush's side of the story, VandeHei says "…with all due respect to our former First Lady, the question I asked, not shouted, seemed very important then and now. It was basically 'How can you come here to Egypt to promote democracy while standing next to the wife of Mr. Mubarak, who is known to be using violence and threats to stamp out pro-Democracy movements in Egypt?" Jim then concluded "But it was a fun and interesting trip!"

Jim's political editor at the *Post* was John F. Harris. It is here where the idea of launching Politico began in casual conversation between VandeHei, Harris, Mike Allen, who worked for *Time* magazine, and a few others. In November of 2006, VandeHei and Harris left their positions at *The Washington Post* to begin their new venture with the financial backing of Robert L. Allbritton (owner of *The Washington Star* and Allbritton Communications).

VandeHei and Harris both assumed leadership roles in the company they co-founded. Today, VandeHei is President and CEO while Harris is Editor-In-Chief with Robert Allbritton as Publisher. Mike Allen is Chief White House correspondent.

Politico, a company that was newly founded in 2006, has quickly risen to the top of the political pyramid. Their credentials are well respected by politicians and media moguls alike. Their list of network appearances is numerous, providing political analysis on all four national networks and cable news channels like MSNBC's *Morning Joe*.

In 2009, VandeHei was selected to serve on the prestigious board of the Pulitzer Prize of American journalism as the very first representative for online news organizations.

The premise, in which the new company was founded upon, brought a new, fresh face to Washington politics. Over the past few decades, politics had become all about opposing Washington. Public sentiment about the government had grown to believe that the federal government was totally ineffective and grossly out of touch. Media coverage, both network and cable, seemed to take a left or right approach, leaving the public with slanted viewpoints and biased, nonobjective analysis. The public was famished for a media source that didn't thrive on escalating the clash over opposing sides, wanting fact based information presented in a way they could form their own opinions.

Politico was created to be a media company that did just that. VandeHei, Harris, and Allen were small town boys who rose to political heights with prestigious media sources like *The Washington Post, The New York Times, The Wall Street Journal,* and *Time* magazine. Their experience gave them the political clout and influence with Washington politicians that provided access to inside information. This access was earned through trust and confidence gained through years of experience and interaction. As the saying goes, "timing is everything." This new media model comes on the cusp of the decline of print media which over time has earned a reputation for the casual "shrug of the shoulders" type of reporting and with the onset of the internet, no longer considered the major source for news. At Politico, the belief is you cannot get quality journalism if you're pushing coverage to the left or right.

As Politico's reputation started to spread, their exposure quickly reached new heights. In 2008, Jim and the Politico team co-moderated with MSNBC and CNN two televised debates during the Presidential campaign, including the first debate to incorporate questions voted on by a live online audience.

In spring of 2011, Jim was awarded an honorary doctorate (Doctorate of Humane Letters, honoris causa) by the University of Wisconsin – Oshkosh for innovative leadership with significant contributions to the University, region, state, and nation. UW Oshkosh Chancellor Richard Wells stated VandeHei is recognized for seizing opportunities and championing new ways to grow two distinct organizations into forces for a more informed and empowered democracy.

In addition to his extremely busy schedule at Politico, Jim finds time to travel across the US to perform public and personal speaking engagements of which he is in high demand. In addition to providing political analysis to the national media, Politico insights are supplied through their monthly magazine, a newspaper, a subscription based newsletter called Politico Pro that is specific to business and industry segments, and of course their website (www.politico.com).

Jim returns home to Oshkosh a few times a year. He and his wife Autumn have two children, Sophie and James, and live in Alexandria, Virginia. Still a devout Green Bay Packers fan, Jim enjoys fishing and getting together with family in their second home in upstate Maine. When Jim is asked about his roots he makes a point to be clear that he graduated from the University of Wisconsin – Oshkosh. He takes constant ribbing from his colleagues about his "Wisconsin accent" and grammar. Using terms like "going to get a drink from the bubbler" or "go down to the stop-n-go lights" usually bring a sideways glance or chuckle from those who know of his Wisconsin upbringing. MSNBC's Joe Scarborough enjoys teasing Jim "on the air" about his native home of Oshkosh.

Just recently, Jim's mother Joan was celebrating a landmark birthday. To mark the occasion, Jim leaned on his network of contacts and convinced some of Washington's elite to agree to tape a birthday greeting for his mom. The special greeting on DVD was played at Joan's birthday celebration in Oshkosh. The first of well-wishes came from her daughter-in-law Autumn, and grandchildren, Sophie and James, wishing her a happy birthday. This was followed by personal greetings from Wisconsin Rep. Paul Ryan, former US Senator Herb Kohl and US Senator Ron Johnson, former Vice President Dick Cheney, and Joe Scarborough, Mika Brzezinski, and Willie Geist from MSNBC's *Morning Joe*. The VIP list of birthday greetings kept growing...former Presidential candidate Ron Paul, ABC's Diane Sawyer, Wolf Blitzer from CNN, and former Governor and Presidential candidate Mitt Romney added their well wishes along with Green Bay Packers players Charles Woodson and Greg Jennings. It was a birthday celebration Joan VandeHei will never forget.

It's uncertain where Jim VandeHei will be in five or ten years from now. Though one thing is for sure...he will always be proud to tell anyone and everyone... "I'm from Oshkosh Wisconsin".

Author's Note: Breaking news - December 2014, Politico announces their entrance into the European political arena with the acquisition of the Belgium based publication *European Voice*. The publication will be rebranded as *Politico* in 2015 and give the company the base to become the leading media player in European politics.

Source: Personal interviews w/ John and Joan VandeHei; www.politico.com; Vanity Fare, Aug. 2009; Washingtonian Magazine, Aug. 2009; UW Oshkosh Today, May 3, 2011; personal correspondence from Jim VandeHei, December 2014;

THE PARANORMAL SIDE OF OSHKOSH
STORIES OF "STRANGE, BUT TRUE" EVENTS...BELIEVE IT, OR NOT!

para·nor·mal

adjective \,pa-rə-`nȯr-məl,\ : *very strange and not able to be explained by what scientists know about nature and the world*

It is no deep dark secret that there are in fact strange things going on in and around the city of Oshkosh and vicinity. In this chapter, I would like to share a few stories that I have heard first-hand from friends and acquaintances; and some that have been published in books, newspapers or on the internet. Some of these stories take place in the city of Oshkosh while others occurred in the immediate surrounding areas.

Deb Daubert

To assist in the writing of this chapter, I would like to introduce Deb Daubert, Curator at the Oshkosh Public Museum. As you would imagine, Deb has a strong passion for local history. As a pastime, she also has a personal interest in paranormal activities. Recently, I invited Deb to work on this project with me to which she enthusiastically agreed. The following short stories are a compilation of our combined efforts to show you a side of Oshkosh you may not have seen, heard of, or experienced before.

Some of you will believe these stories to be true. Others may scoff and turn a skeptical or cynical eye to these strange happenings. Whether you believe them or not, is entirely up to you. But the next time you are lying awake and cannot sleep, when suddenly you hear a noise…what will you imagine? Will you just brush it off as the house settling? Perhaps it is just the furnace kicking in. Or, might it be something else?

So, grab your Ouija® board and join us on a journey into the mysterious side of life around Oshkosh. Be prepared for a truly spirited adventure…

The Abominable Snowman
by Randy Domer

Some call it *The Abominable Snowman*. Others refer to it as a *Sasquatch or Yeti*.

Not far from Oshkosh, in the northwest corner of Winnebago County, stands a marshy area that covers several square miles. In one regard, the marsh is a unique place because it consists of a special kind of natural grass. During the early part of the twentieth century a local Oshkosh company would harvest this special grass and use it to weave rugs. The Deltox Company was located on Wisconsin Ave, adjacent to the Fox River. Grass was harvested from this marsh, which became known to locals as the *Deltox Marsh*. Grass rugs were woven from this "wire grass" as it was known. Crews of workers would harvest the grass and press it into bales. The bales were then hauled by teams of horses to the Wolf River east of Fremont where they would be loaded onto the steamboat *Leander Choate* and shipped to the rug company in Oshkosh.

But another little known incident occurred here that makes it even more unique. It was near this Deltox Marsh on October 19, 1968 that three men ventured in for a day of bow hunting whitetail deer. They had just begun to make their way to their deer stands. As the trio walked into the acres of tall grass, they suddenly spotted something unusual. Catching only a glimpse as the object moved quickly away, the hunters were unsure what to make of what they just saw. At first thinking it was a hunter dressed in unusual garb or maybe even a bear, the men quickly dismissed the latter as the legs were too long for a bear.

The men went on with their hunt that day with no further incident.

These same three hunters returned with a group of nine others in November and that is when the second sighting occurred. The group was making a "drive" through the marsh hoping to arouse deer from their marshy hiding places and bedding grounds. One of the hunters decided to climb a nearby tree to attempt to gain a better view of the huge swamp that spans about eight square miles.

As the group proceeded into the marsh, three men on the left flank of the line, looking ahead, spotted a strange looking creature standing upright. The grass was estimated to be three to four feet in height, and the creature's torso was clearly visible above it. Because of its man-like appearance they did not shoot. The creature then walked quickly away, stopping to look back each time the men stopped walking. Eventually, it disappeared into a nearby thicket.

The creature was described as being a broad-shouldered, barrel-shaped body with black or brownish hair about four inches in length. It's face and palms were bare and the legs and arms unusually long.

The hunters reported their experience to the local game warden and word soon spread. The Science Editor of *Argosy Magazine* became interested after reading the story in the local newspaper, the *Oshkosh Daily Northwestern*.

A "Yeti Hunt" was scheduled for a Saturday afternoon in December. VIPs from New York television and magazines traveled through a blizzard as they drove from New Jersey to Wisconsin to participate in the event. The event was covered locally by Green Bay's *WLUK TV 11* with sports reporter Al Sampson doing the coverage. The group met at the nearby Orihula Resort before heading out.

The creature was not sighted that day; however tracks were discovered measuring seventeen inches in length and a depth of the impression that estimated the creature weighed around 400 pounds.

Publications are listed below as sources for this story, and list the following names as witnesses:

The first three bow hunters were: Dick Bleier, Bill Mallo and Bob Parry.

Joining these three in November were: Dick Tellock, Richard Vanderberg, Pete Vanderberg, Kurt Krueger, Artie Tellock, Lester Zuehlke, Don Svacina, Romy Svacina and an unidentified man from Milwaukee.

Authors note: My favorite deer hunting spot was located about ten miles from this location, and I hunted there from 1966 to 2009. When I think back about walking to my deer stand in the dark at 5:30am, I would imagine the noises I heard along the trail, a twig snap, a rustling in the pines…must be spooking deer. Now I'm not so sure.

Sources: Fremont-Wolf River Area History, Fremont, Wis. Area Bi-Centennial Committee; Monsters of Wisconsin: Mysterious Creatures in the Badger State, Linda S. Godfrey

Lake Winnebago or Loch Ness?
By Randy Domer

We have all heard tales about the mysterious creature that allegedly lurks in the depths of Loch Ness in Scotland. Did you know at one time, Lake Winnebago had a mysterious creature of its own?

This story comes from an article (Letter to the Editor) published in the *Oshkosh Daily Northwestern* on August 7, 1876. The text is taken verbatim from the article.

The Sea Lion

A Party Claims to Have Seen the Monster – A Whaling Voyage on Lake Winnebago

To the Editor of the Northwestern.

A party of gentlemen from the Revere House started yesterday morning for a trip on the lake to Garlick Island on the steamer O.B. Reed. When about three miles from Oshkosh some of the party who were standing on the bow of the boat, saw a dark object in the water about a half a mile in front of them, headed for the shore, and as none of the party could make out what it was the steamer was headed for it. When she was about two hundred yards from the object it disappeared beneath the water. The steamer was immediately stopped and all hands were on the lookout its reappearance. In a few moments one of

the party called out "there it is!" and sure enough within one hundred and fifty yards of the steamer, making towards the shore we saw Cooper and Baily's Sea Lion that escaped from them here a short time since. Then visions of the $500 reward began to float before the eyes of all on board. In a moment the small boat was lowered and into it was thrown some rope, boat hooks, oars and an old shotgun belonging to Capt. Reed. The Captain called for volunteers to assist him in the capture of the monster and although all of us would have been glad to have had a hand in the matter it was impossible, as the boat was only large enough to carry three persons comfortably. So Capt. Reed selected Mr. Geo. W. Hart of New York and Mr. Geo. Cameron the genial host of the Revere House to go with him. Their coats and vests were off in a moment, into the boat they jumped and began pulling in the direction of the monster amid cries of caution from those left on board the steamer. Mr. Cameron occupied the bow of the boat, Mr. Hart sat in the stern and with an oar directed its course. Capt. Reed was the propelling power at the oars. When we were about twenty yards from the creature, it disappeared, but this time only for a moment when it was again seen by those on the steamer to be seemingly only within an arms length of the small boat and directly in front of it we saw Mr. Cameron raise a boat hook and strike the monster a fearful blow on the head, but unfortunately it only seemed to have the effect of enraging it, and we were horrified to see him raise a part of his body from the water and descending strike the side of the boat with his jaws, crushing it as if it were an eggshell, throwing the occupants into the water. There was a cry of horror raised from the steamer as we saw the brave men sink but, in a moment they arose and we saw them strike out for the wrecked boat. Capt. Reed being the elder of the party was last to reach it, and Mr. Hart and Mr. Cameron extended each a hand, helping him onto the boat which lay bottom up. The steamer was immediately headed for them, and just in time; for as we got near to them, we saw the creature rise again but a few yards away. But seeing the steamer he turned and swam out into the lake disappearing in a few moments. We took the three men on board, none the worse, except for the wetting, for their bath. After cruising about for at least an hour and seeing nothing of the lion we gave up the chase and returned home feeling we had lost five hundred dollars.
(signed) No Joking

Author's Note: The Cooper and Bailey Circus formed in the 1860s by James A. Bailey and James E. Cooper. They soon became the chief competitor to PT Barnum. Bailey is reported to be the first to display an electric light a year before Thomas Edison patented it. My research on the internet verified <u>The Cooper and Bailey Circus visited Oshkosh on August 1, 1876</u>. Soon after, Barnum and Bailey decided it was better to work together than compete and five years later they combined shows with Barnum enjoying great success. Barnum died in 1891 and Bailey purchased the circus from Barnum's widow. In 1907, The Ringling Brothers purchased the Barnum and Bailey Circus and the new company was known as Ringling Brothers and Barnum and Bailey Combined Shows, the Greatest Show on Earth.

Sources: wisconsinhistory.org/topics/ringlingbros; circushistory.org/ Routes/CB 1876.htm; www.elephant.se

The Beckwith House

by Deb Daubert

The Northwest corner of Algoma Boulevard and Main Street in downtown Oshkosh has long held a reputation of ghostly activity. Numerous stories abound of people witnessing ghostly figures, items unexplainably flying through the air and sometimes a general feeling of creepiness. Searching for the possible basis of such claims can easily be found by knowing the tragic history of that corner. However, who might be causing all the rumpus is open to conjecture with plenty of contenders.

The spring and summer of 1875 experienced especially dry conditions causing several bad fires and leaving downtown Oshkosh in ruins. Sanford Beckwith, who lost his hotel in that fire, was determined to rebuild bigger and more elegant than Oshkosh had ever seen before and enlisted the help of architect William Waters. By June of 1876, after many delays and code disputes, his new enterprise, the Beckwith House, was completed. The main entrance of the hotel opened onto

Main Street, where patrons encountered a staircase which took them up to the large and luxurious lobby on the second floor. This same floor included an office with adjacent space for maintenance, two large parlors with balconies overlooking Main Street, a men's lounge, a large dining room able to hold one hundred and fifty diners, restrooms of marble and silver-plated fixtures, a modern kitchen, and sample rooms where salesman could exhibit their products. Another set of winding stairs went to the sleeping accommodations on the third and fourth floors. No expense was spared to create an imposing first-class hotel. Beneath the hotel, at street level, the first floor held many businesses.

The hotel flourished as its reputation for excellence grew, soon making it the setting for Oshkosh society. That is, until December 3, 1880 when an event took place that shocked the community and made the national newspapers. Tragedy struck as a bellboy named Rogers was tackling his daily routine of cleaning and replenishing the kerosene lamps used to light the rooms of the hotel. Suddenly, one of the lamps exploded throwing burning kerosene around the room, turning it quickly into an inferno. The room's location under the stairs leading to the third and fourth floor acted as a chimney, carrying the flames rapidly upward, and closing off the main route of escape. It was reported that the fire spread so quickly that the hotel was completely engulfed in flames before any alarm could be given to the occupants of the building.

Considering the death-trap created due to the route of the conflagration, it is amazing that only three individuals lost their lives. Nevertheless, the circumstances surrounding their demise may account for certain bizarre occurrences within the businesses since housed in the shell of what once was the first and second floors of the Beckwith House.

Mr. and Mrs. Simon Paige occupied one of the finest suite of rooms. Instead of owning their own home, the extremely wealthy Oshkosh couple had retained rooms in the hotel since it was built. However they were rarely there, enjoying traveling around the world together. Due to earlier encounters with fires, Mrs. Paige was especially fearful of being trapped by one and had made arrangements with the night watchman and porter, George Wood, to help her escape if the situation warranted it. Mr. Paige had spent years trying to convince Mr. Beckwith to install fire escapes and after receiving no results had rigged up his own system with ropes which were always kept ready by the couple.

The Beckwith House stands in all its glory in early 1880.

Photos Courtesy of Dan Radig

A shell is all that remains of the Beckwith House following the tragic fire of 1880.

Photos Courtesy of Dan Radig

On that fateful day, Mrs. Paige had just welcomed her friend, Mrs. Harmon, for a little gossip before they were to join friends for tea. Hearing much commotion from within the hotel and finally a call of fire, the two women attempted to flee the room, only to discover the escape route through the halls was impassable. Retreating back to the Paige's suite of rooms, the women found it filling with thick black smoke and flames bursting through the walls. Running to the windows the frantic ladies looked down to find firemen holding blankets and a crowd yelling Jump! Jump! Mrs. Harmon almost crazed by fright did just that and although gravely injured by the fall survived. The crowd now anxiously watched for any sign of Mrs. Paige and Mr. Paige frantically offered a reward for anyone who would bring her out alive. After a couple of failed attempts fire fighter Charles Rief was able to enter the room by the open window. There on the floor lay Mrs. Paige, who Rief claimed was still alive but badly injured. Fixing a rope around her, she was lowered, with much difficulty, to the ground and then transported by carriage to the home of John Paige where she was pronounced dead.

Is it possible that Mrs. Paige still roams the halls of the former Beckwith House...awaiting her rescue?

George Wood, the night watchman and porter who Mrs. Paige had counted on to come to her aid, was found to be missing after the fire was extinguished. George Wood was an African American of about thirty-years-old, who had been born in Canada. Thought to be industrious, prudent and of good habits (especially known for not drinking) he was much respected in Oshkosh. Bad health had forced him around 1878 to quit his job as a Pullman sleeping car porter between Chicago and San Francisco on the Central Pacific Railroad. Thinking outside employment might help his health, he tried working for a farmer in Sheboygan County and Ingram's Livery in Fond du Lac before settling in at the Beckwith House.

Being a night watchman and porter meant George Wood usually slept during daylight hours, but on the day of the fire he had a severe toothache and could not sleep. He talked about going to get his tooth pulled but finally his courage failed him and he instead was induced to take some laudanum (an alcoholic extract of opium which was legal and commonly used at the time). Some thought he may have become insensible due to the potency of the narcotic and suffocated in bed. However, when they searched the rubble directly below his room, only his pocket watch, but no body, was found. All sorts of rumors surfaced. It wasn't until January 18, 1881 that the remains of George Wood were found by workmen clearing the ruins. His body, with a half burnt rope coiled around it, was directly under what would have been a few feet from Mrs. Paige's door.

Perhaps George Wood's ghostly presence is an endeavor to keep his promise to rescue Mrs. Paige.

Twenty-five year old Mary "Mollie" Hanrahan was one of the most popular dining room servers at the hotel, known for her smiling face and pleasant word for all. Born and raised in Scott, located in Manitowoc County Wisconsin, Mollie had come to Oshkosh to find work. She was employed at the Revere House when in 1877 it mysteriously burnt to the ground. Mollie, along with the other servants there, narrowly escaped by sliding down the roof of a nearby shed. Mollie, only saving the nightgown she wore, was given shelter at the Beckwith House and then employment later. Mollie again found herself fortunate the day of the Beckwith fire. She had safely made her way outside the burning building, when she suddenly turned, as if remembering something important, and reentered the burning building. Two other girls working their way down the narrow back stairs implored her to leave with them, but Mollie seemed determined to recover something. The last anyone saw of her she was bending over her trunk which was by her sewing machine. Mollie's body was later recovered under the back staircase, buried in the debris along with her trunk. It was speculated that she was trying to drag it down the steps when the smoke overcame her. Friends claimed Mollie had saved $250 of her wages which were stored in the demolished trunk.

Is it possible Mollie is still looking for her lost wages?

Whether this corner retains the spirits of these three souls or has gathered others to its halls will remain a mystery until one of them decides to reveal who they are.

Sources: www.oshkoshmuseum.org online archival collection; *Oshkosh Northwestern* articles: 6/24/1876, 1/17/1877, 1/20/1877, 6/24/1879, 12/4/1880, 12/6/1880, 1/20/1881, 7/4/1914 and 11/14/1934; Oshkosh City Directories from 1876, 1879 and 1880; Ancestry.com for Mrs. Paige, George Wood and Mollie Hanrahan; http://williamwatersoshkosharchitect.blogspot.com/2013_08_01_archive.html

The Grand Opera House
by Randy Domer and Deb Daubert

One of the most famous haunts in Oshkosh is the historic Grand Opera House. Built in 1883, the Grand was considered one of the finest theaters north of Milwaukee. Its stages were graced by famous actors, musicians, comedians, magicians, vaudevillians and even President William Howard Taft. Over the years, the opera house went through many transitions. In the 1950s it was a movie theater and at one time, during the lowest point of its life, an X-Rated movie house.

In the 1980s renovations were executed through the effort of a strong community based organization to bring the old building back to its glory days. Years of meticulous renovation slowly showed Oshkosh what the beautiful old building was like during its prime.

Little did we know, however, that all the work, construction, noise, tearing down walls would awaken the spirits of The Grand. It seems Oshkosh has its own "Phantom of the Opera".

The spirit that most frequents this haunted old building is Percy Keene, former stage manager for The Grand. Percy worked in the theater from 1895 until his death in 1967. Shortly after his death, the first of many sightings of the former stage man were reported. Later in 1976, a group of UWO students were filming a television movie, *Exit Dying,* inside the theater. During the filming, unusual activities seemed to escalate, causing some to speculate Mr. Keene did not approve of what was going on. Some of the students claimed to have seen a man with round glasses smiling at them from the balcony. As they described the man in more detail, it was clear the ghost they saw was that of Percy Keene.

On another occasion, a student was allegedly kept from falling when a rope broke but was held together by an entity of some sort (believed to be Percy) and during the sneak preview of the film Percy was once again spotted standing in the balcony. One evening, a member of the filming cast was walking outside the theater after it was closed when he noticed a man looking down at him through the window. Thinking he was a night watchman, he mentioned this the next day to theater management, only to discover the Grand had no night watchman.

Footsteps are sometimes heard climbing the balcony steps, but no one is there. There are also reports of a dog that roams the theater, sometimes surprising and frightening guests. Actors and employees of the century old theater have seen what they call apparitions in the basement below the stage. One lady claimed someone grabbed her ankle and another told of seeing a man in the Orchestra Pit leave through a doorway. When the door was checked, the room was empty.

The Oshkosh Advance-Titan reported in their November 30, 1978 edition, the existence of a canine presence. The article claims the theater is haunted by a dog which died in the basement of the old opera house years ago. Some people have reported hearing a dog barking in the theater late at night.

A front row seat, specifically seat 1-A in the orchestra level left, has been known to move up and down as though someone is sitting in it. The seat cushion even flattened as though the weight of a person is there, waiting for the performance to begin.

The basement area is where you would expect to house a restless spirit. Very low ceilings with rooms packed full of equipment like chairs, stage props, lighting paraphernalia and other assorted theater items. Walking through the labyrinth beneath the ground, one imagines the possibility of tunnels that were rumored to network underground to places unknown. The most popular belief connects one of the tunnels to the old Athearn Hotel that was located across the street. Was there such a tunnel network? If so, where did they go and what secrets would they hold?

I recently talked with Vivian Hazell who was employed at the Grand in the 1990s as the Hospitality Coordinator. Her duties included attending to the needs of visiting performers during their stay and performance. Because of her responsibilities, she was required to sometimes enter the theater during non-regular business hours, when no one else was around, and so she had a key to access the building.

On one occasion, she was making a delivery and parked at the rear of the building where she had easy access to the side door which led through the basement into the dressing room area. She then went on to explain what happened next. "I needed to make three trips to unload everything I had. The first two trips through the basement were just fine. I walked through the storage area where a clear path took me to my destination on the opposite side of the room. I was making my third and final trip when I discovered something disturbing. As I entered the basement, the clear path I had used previously was now cluttered with props, trunks, and even pink flamingos strewn about, now blocking my way. As I was alone in the building, my mind quickly realized there was no reasonable explanation. I high-tailed it out of there and left."

Still not a believer? Maybe a chat with Joe Ferlo, the Executive Director of the Grand will convince you. Ferlo has been receiving reports like this for years. Each October, Ferlo and his cast of actors, volunteers and staff members host the Haunted Grand tours. Guests are invited to hear the history behind the old theater, then led on a tour that illustrates through actors, some of the strange things that occurred here. In 2013, I decided to take the tour and found it fun, interesting and even a little spooky. Perhaps a tour in October will convince you to believe.

So, the next time you visit the Grand for a performance, before you sit down, you may want to ask "Is this seat taken?"

Sources: www.hauntedhouses.com/states/wi/opera_house; www. prairieghosts.com; http://www.imdb.com/title/tt3521172/

The Winter of the West Algoma Phantom
by Deb Daubert

A "terrifying specter that haunted West Algoma" had long been forgotten by area residents until it was featured in the 1958 folklore issue of the Wisconsin State Historical Society's monthly pamphlet *Wisconsin Then and Now*.

To set the stage for this local haunting the location and time of year play key roles.

The location was the old West Algoma section of Oshkosh. (Basically west of the Fox River, land around Sawyer Avenue, Highway 21 and along the South shore of Lake Butte des Morts.) The area was once inhabited by Native Americans and it was the location of the historic Knaggs Ferry in Oshkosh. This edge of Oshkosh was quite rural, attracting prominent men such as Philetus Sawyer and Governor Bashford along with workers whose names are long forgotten, making the neighborhood an interesting blend of Yankee entrepreneurs and common laborers. In 1892 it was reported to have roughly eighty-two homes and eight business buildings.

During the long, cold winter months was when the majority of the men in West Algoma left home for several months to work in the north woods logging. It was essential to do logging during the cold months of the year to take advantage of icy pathways needed to help horses and oxen move huge sleighs piled high with large and heavy timber. These loads would be moved to the nearest water source like the Wolf River where water from spring thaws would take over transporting the logs south to the mills.

The haunting, according to the folklore article, happened around the winter of 1894 when most of the men had left for the woods, leaving a population consisting mainly of women and children. That is why the sudden appearance of a "person" of fabulous height covered by a long black cape walking the street every night around midnight was said to have caused such fear and panic. The phantom's slow, measured footsteps could be clearly heard in the winter night as he tread the wooden planked sidewalks. When he reached the end of the walk, all would go silent and he would disappear into the blackness of the night.

But neither the story nor the suspense stopped there, for without fail, one and a half hours later the specter would reappear to follow the course in reverse only to disappear in the opposite direction. This routine never varied in time, manner or location making the residents extremely anxious over what was yet to come. No one in the entire community was willing to interfere with this schedule, yet they never slept until the bizarre ritual was completed. Then spring arrived, the men returned from the north woods and the preambles of the phantom stopped, never to return. What better proof that something paranormal had occurred.

Shortly after this tale appeared in 1958, several West Algoma pioneer families exchanged correspondence over this tale. Interestingly enough, no one remembered such a specter, or any other for that matter, haunting the neighborhood during their youth. On comparing notes, speculation was made on how certain facts may have been exaggerated over the years.

The only person who ever walked at night and in such a manner that anyone remembered personally or heard another family member talk about was a long way from a phantom. He was in fact, a priest from the Alexian Hospital which was on the corner of New York and Jackson Avenues. The midnight hour and precise timing was explained by one submitter who claimed the priest traveled part of the way by street car while others suggested the priest just waited until late at night when no one was around. The fact that he disappeared was just an illusion caused by the black-color of his priestly raiment against the dark of night. Since it was winter, and weather reports from 1892-1894 claimed more snow than usual, the priest is reported to have worn a huge scarf over his hooded cossack-clad shoulders and wrapped around his face, making him appear faceless. The coloring of his garb also gave the appearance of a wicked black phantom to those who associated ghostly attire properly being a white shroud. The slow measured tread was due to the priest's failing health and the assistance of a cane. Finally, the fact that the midnight walks stopped when the men returned from the logging camps never to happen again, coincided with the death of the priest.

Sources: *Oshkosh Northwestern* 2/10/1893, 2/14/1893; History-Review-Story: Dedicated to the Pioneers of the old West Algoma and Vicinity, 1957 by Edward W. Freda; Addendum West Algoma History, 1959 by Edward W. Freda; Ancestry.com; www.oshkoshmuseum.org, online archival photograph collection; http://www. wisconsinhistory.org /history of logging and folklore; http://www.wisconsin trails.com/culture/Logging-history-runs-deep-in-Wisconsins-Northwoods-268493232.html ; http://recollectionwisconsin.org/lumber-camp-life

Grandma's Ghost

by Randy Domer

This story was provided to me by a good friend who has lived in Oshkosh his entire life and is now retired. As he has requested anonymity, I will refer to him as "Walter". In my years of knowing Walter, I never knew him to be one to talk about the "spirit world" or even hint that he might believe in the supernatural or paranormal activities. That is why I was slightly taken aback when one day he chose to share an experience with me that happened to him several years ago.

The waiting area after the dance review was filled with family members waiting for their children who had just finished performing. Being very social, it wasn't long before Walter struck up a conversation with some folks standing nearby. (For the sake of confidentiality, let's call these folks Betty and Bob). As small talk goes, one thing led to another when Betty and Bob revealed they had at one time lived on Monroe Street. After more prodding and probing, Walter was astonished to discover they had once lived in the house of his late grandmother.

The conversation was going well, that is until Bob and Betty revealed some of the strange things that occurred while they lived there. "There were some weird things going on there that kind of gave us the creeps," Betty said. "One time, there were some books lying on the kitchen counter. Suddenly, they went flying across the room!" she exclaimed.

Her comment chilled Walter to the bone. He then informed them "I lived with my grandmother there for some time, and she had a few rules. When we came home from school, as kids would do, we sometimes placed our books on the kitchen counter. My grandmother stated in no uncertain terms that was not the place for school books and made us move them." Both Walter and his new acquaintances were taken aback by this revelation.

Then Betty shared another instance they couldn't explain. "Our bedroom was on the second floor, accessible by a set of old, creaky, wooden stairs. On occasion, after we had turned in for the night, we would hear footsteps coming up the stairs. It sounded like the person would take a step, then bring their other foot along, climbing the stairs one step at a time. When we investigated, there was no one there."

Now Walter was shaken by this recent incident. "My grandmother climbed the stairs that way...one step at a time because of her age."

They also told Walter that on another occasion, they came downstairs one morning and found all the doors to the built-in China cabinet were wide open.

The experience left Walter filled with questions and the feeling of uneasiness.

At this point, it was time to leave. Walter thanked Betty and Bob and exchanged pleasantries as they departed. The experience for Walter left an indelible memory that has him wondering if his grandmother may still have some type of earthly connection. The answer is out there somewhere...

Jefferson Street Hijinks
by Deb Daubert

One residential street in Oshkosh, not known as a major transportation route, may nevertheless be a busy thoroughfare for otherworldly beings. For the past one hundred and thirty years, Jefferson Street has repeatedly appeared in reports of spirited activity.

One such account emerged on October 8, 1887 in the *Oshkosh Northwestern*. People living near a house on Oshkosh's Jefferson Street reported that at the "dreaded hour of midnight, strange sounds could be heard coming from the house" as well as the "curious actions of pieces of furniture supposed to be influenced by some supernatural power." Several families had attempted to live in the house, but all moved out claiming to be afraid to stay after dark. Only J. E. Brown and his family declared they did not experience any of the activity related while they lived in the house. Well-known African-American Oshkosh citizens, J. E. and his wife ran a barber shop and Turco-Russian, magnetic and electric bath room business on Main Street. Whatever their denials to witnessing any paranormal activities, the family soon moved out claiming the location was not convenient to work nor the furnishings to their liking.

A possible explanation behind why the house was haunted appeared several days later in the same newspaper. Neighbors reported seeing a man who would visit the site every night around midnight. It was suggested he created the commotion in an effort to depreciate the property's value. The newspaper then passed along a message from the real-estate agent selling the house that if the eerie activity did not cease he would personally "convert the live ghost into a corpse unless he quit visiting the house." Subsequently, no further reports on this haunting were found.

One of the most infamous acts that took place in Oshkosh occurred on Jefferson Street and may have also included an actual haunting. Breaking news in the Monday, April 25, 1898 edition of the *Oshkosh Northwestern* was of two people shot early Sunday morning in a house on Jefferson Street. The first account of this tragic event stated that the "female inmates" of the dwelling were entertaining "guests" when an argument between a man and woman was heard to break out, ending in gun shots. When the door to the room where the shooting had taken place was broken down, it appeared that forty-year-old Birdie Fox had been shot in a jealous rage by thirty-year-old George Miles before he turned the revolver on himself.

Birdie Fox was around forty years old and according to the newspaper had been "quite handsome years ago" but conceded she was "of fine physique." A short biography followed stating that she had lived in Oshkosh for the past twenty years and before that resided in the country a few miles from town. Her name had "originally been" Blanche Deiter, she had married several times and had "always been law-abiding and conducted herself well for a woman of her class." They also went on to claim she owned considerable property which included the house on Jefferson Street. Since Birdie's exploits over the years, and those of her mother and two sisters, had often been reported in local newspapers (as well as being familiar to the police department) it is debatable on how law-abiding she had been.

When Birdie died of her wounds later that Sunday morning, the coroner's inquest revealed some intriguing evidence. The sworn testimonies of Dr. Corbett, Dr. Oviatt and Dr. Connors, who performed the post mortem on Birdie, concluded that one bullet entered at her breast and traveled downward indicating it had been fired from above. The path of the second bullet which entered her stomach indicated that she must have been in a sitting crouched position. Although only three shots were reported to have been heard, both victims had two wounds and a fifth bullet was found in the wall. Several witnesses also gave evidence that they had heard Miles say after the shooting "Birdie, Birdie, why did you make me do it." The proof and testimonies were conclusive enough to determine that Miles was responsible for the murder of Birdie after which he must have attempted suicide.

But Miles, against all predictions began a slow process of recovery. The more his condition improved, the more the proof and testimonies seemed to change making Birdie the villain and Miles the victim.

In the end, skilled attorneys for the defense helped Miles be acquitted of murder, despite the evidence uncovered by the coroner's inquest and the almost overwhelming odds and popular opinion against him.

As the story and character of Birdie shifted, in January of 1899 a *Milwaukee Journal* article reported evidence of Birdie's posthumous displeasure in how the case was going. "Since her [Birdie Fox] murder last April, the house in which she met her untimely end has been the scene of queer happenings and uncanny festivities. On certain nights, the neighbors say, the rooms blaze up with a myriad of lights from cellar to garret and they are as suddenly extinguished. Again one room will be instantly lighted up and remain illuminated for the whole night. White flitting shadows have been seen to dance before the windows and seem to beckon to the frightened neighbors from the spirit land. No noises ever accompany the ghostly revels..." No explanation or further details could be found on whether the ghostly activity stopped or is still happening today.

Author's Note: Due to no actual haunting being proven, addresses have not been released for these stories. However, several people have shared their stories of possible ghostly experiences while living on this street.

Sources: *Oshkosh Northwestern*: 7/20/1878, 3/26/1886, 7/19/1886, 6/27/1887, 10/8/1887, 10/14/1887, 4/18/1888, 5/23/1888, 4/25/1898, 4/26/1898, 4/27/1898, 4/30/1898, 7/7/1898, 7/29/1898, 8/13/1898, 10/23/1898, 1/7/1899, 1/9/1899, 8/30/1899, 11/14/1899, 11/15/1899, 11/16/1899, 11/17/1899, 11/20/1899; www.oshkoshmuseum.org: online archival photograph collection; Ancestry.com; census information on Birdie Fox/Blanche Deiter and George Miles

HANKS CLUB

This story was given to me by Oshkosh resident Vern Gauger who has researched and written many topics relative to local history. Verne writes, he claims, more to just get information down before it fades from his memories and of those who lived them. With his expressed permission, the following is written verbatim in Vern's words.

"Henry Misfeldt was a young man who was hospitable, generous and with a little bit of money. He lived on Lake Street in the middle of the "fish district." He liked to fish and he liked company. He, with the help of Ed Kieckhaefer, purchased a 90 x 90 foot lot on the lake [Lake Winnebago] at the foot of Waugoo on which he built a small house.

Henry invited some of the neighborhood guys, fellows who shared some of his interests; fishing, playing cards, smoking, drinking, shooting the breeze. The year was 1892.

In 1904 a club was formed with the men who frequented the premises on a regular basis. They called the club The Dozen Club although by the end of the year membership stood at 20.

The membership fee was $10.00 and dues were 25¢ a month. The club purchased "merchandise" for resale to members and sold it at minimum markup: beer, whiskey, brandy, cigarettes and soda. All sales were labeled "donations" so that the Club would not be considered a business. In the early years the most frequent purchases seemed to be playing cards and matches. Dues and "donations" allowed the Club to operate and pay bills for the necessities like wood, kerosene and Real Estate Taxes.

In the early years, few records were kept, some were lost or misplaced, some illegible, unclear or confusing. However, the Club continued to function without much need to keep records. In fact, in

1924 an addition was built on the clubhouse and a kitchen was added. The whole structure was wired for electricity. A new boathouse and dock were added. Members did all the work and the only cost to the Club was for building materials. If record keeping was not one of their strong suits, one record was religiously kept, that of keeping track of the date the ice "went out" of the lake. The record keeping originated in 1909 and has been posted on the clubhouse wall every year since. Extra informational comments were sometimes added, for instance: 1923, February 11, lightning and heavy rain, temperature 58 degrees; 1920-1921, warmest on record, ice 16" thick, March 11 first day of snow, March 19, ice breaking up; 1931-1932 lake open until January 22, January 28-29 8 below, mild winter, digging angle worms on January 24.

Purchases made by members,(beer, whiskey, cigarettes, etc.), was on the honor system. Members served themselves and it was expected that when they took something out of inventory they would pay the established price and put the money in the till.

In the 1920s during prohibition, moonshine was made in the club by members, but since it was made for members' consumption only, everyone assumed that it was within the law.

The Club survived for years but with declining membership. It seemed that Hank would be the sole survivor of a "Last Man's Club".

In 1959, Hank met with some of the men who attended meetings regularly and who seemed to be interested in continuing the relationship. Hank offered to turn over the land and the clubhouse to a new club which was to be formed at the time of the transfer. Hank wished that the new club would be a limited, continuous membership so that when a member died or resigned from the club, the club membership would replace him with another suitable member.

And so, on January 1, 1960, the Henry Misfeldt Lakeshore Recreation Club LTD was officially formed with the assistance of attorney Bill Crane.

The indenture recorded the payment of One Dollar to Henry Misfeldt and was signed by nine members and (strangely enough) eight wives. Those signing the indenture were Henry Misfeldt, Carl Fiebig, Tom Pamplin, Donald Schutz, Robert Kliforth, Edwin Luther, Arden Gauger and Alfred Madaus.

It was stipulated that if the club should ever disband, the property would be sold and the proceeds would be distributed one-half to Mercy Hospital and one-half to the Salvation Army.

The first meeting of the new club was held January 3, 1960. Nineteen members were in attendance. Election of officers was held and Henry Misfeldt was elected President, Tom Pamplin – First Vice President, Frank Schreiber – Second Vice President, Ed Luther – Secretary, and Earl Disch – Treasurer. The President nominated 5 members for the Board of Directors: Ed Luther – Chairman, Al Madaus, Harold Riedi, Vernon Frohrib and Arden Gauger.

Meetings were to be held on the first Tuesday of each month and election of officers at the December meeting."

-Vern Gauger

Author's Note: Hank's Club still resides in its original location at 1372 Waugoo Avenue in Oshkosh on the shores of beautiful Lake Winnebago. As of November, 2014 the officers of the club include: Kevin Seifeldt-President, Bill Runke-Vice President, Tom Anfinson-Secretary, Milt Schafer-Treasurer. Board members are Dave Jantz, Broc Miller, Jeff Ruck, Jeff Steinert, Taylor Steinert and Fran Tomaschefski.

According to board member Jeff Steinert, club membership includes 40 paying members and 12 honorary members (members that have reached age 60 and have been a member for at least 25 years). Hank's Club has a closed membership system. New members are nominated by club members and the new member's name is read in to the record at three consecutive monthly meetings, after which at the third and final reading is voted on by members in attendance. Membership is limited to 40 paying members.

Monies collected by the club are used to support Club activities such as summer and winter fisherees and during the summer months, Friday Fish Frys. Revenues are also used for building maintenance, and to pay utilities, taxes, etc.

Today, Hank's Club continues as a long standing tradition which began with Henry Misfeldt's dream over a hundred years ago!

THE AXLE
BY JAMES SENDERHAUF

I walked into the building at 1005 High Avenue on a warm night in May of 1963. I was hired for common labor on the night shift (11pm. to 7am). It was supposed to be a summer job before I went back to college. I retired and walked out after working there for 43 years and was the Manufacturing Manager. Before I get too far I think the story has to start with the history.

The History

People who never worked at the Axle may not realize that the huge conglomerate called Rockwell International, (according to the Forbes 500, at one time the 27th largest Corporation in the world), had its start in 1919 at what is now 1005 High Avenue. The Rockwell family lived in Oshkosh. From this humble beginning, Willard F. Rockwell merged and bought many companies. He and his engineers designed and patented the planetary axle which was the lifeblood of the Oshkosh plant. There were many name changes[1] over the years but the location was always the same.

Wisconsin Parts (1919)
Timken Detroit Axle and Wisconsin Axle (1929)
Rockwell Spring and Axle (1953)
Rockwell Standard (1958)
North American Rockwell (1967)
Rockwell International (1973)
Meritor® (1997)

ArvinMeritor® (2000)
AxleTech® International (2002)
AxleTech® (Carlyle Group) (2005)
AxleTech® (General Dynamics) (2008)
AxleTech® (Carlyle Group) (2015)

Being under the corporate umbrella of Rockwell International was prestigious and we were proud employees. It was affectionately known as "The Rock". It was a rock for many of us and we bragged about how they took care of us from "womb to tomb". The automotive division had twelve or thirteen plants in the USA of which Oshkosh was considered the flagship location. Over time, things slowly started to change. In 1997, Rockwell International was downsizing and they spun off their automotive division and we became Meritor and then Arvin-Meritor.

Ownership changes continued over the years until the most recent (2015) transaction saw General Dynamics selling the Oshkosh plant back to Carlyle.

It is important to know that some of these changes were transparent, but others were disruptive. Corporate policies and philosophies changed and the employees had to be able to adjust to these changes. Employees lost jobs over the years. The 1,300 hourly employees and the more than 200 management people, who were there in the peak years of the 1960s, are today a small group of approximately 100 total employees (as of this writing). The 1,000 machines once housed in the 600,000 square foot facility have now been reduced to zero, and assembly is the only manufacturing being performed there. The jury is out on what the next step is for the Oshkosh plant. It would seem so different to ride down High Street in Oshkosh and not see that building there. Hopefully, Carlyle has a plan to bring work in and put some laid-off employees back to work.

The Product

Colonel Rockwell, as he came to be known, came to Oshkosh and patented the double reduction planetary axle. The patent for this axle still hangs in the lobby of the Oshkosh plant. This is not a glamorous product. These are big tough axles, designed to be used under adverse conditions in construction, mines, and military uses and can weigh up to 8,000 pounds each. Some of the smaller axles can be found on the luggage carts used in airports and some of the larger ones are used under cranes. Others are used under cars bringing coal out of mines and some can be found on huge lift trucks, capable of lifting containers loaded for ships or put on flatcars. In addition we made transfer cases, another complicated product, and we made them by the thousands. No matter what other products were being made, the bread and butter was always the planetary axle.

Factory Life

What is it like spending your life in a factory? Entering as a young kid and then retiring as a mature adult, I never intended to spend my working lifetime there. Most of us who worked there probably never did. It just happens. The years go by; you start a family, begin accruing benefits, and end up staying. The Axle was the best place to work in the city. It paid the best, had the best benefits, and we felt fortunate to have a job there. We were proud to say we worked there.

In 1963, when I walked in that door I was apprehensive to say the least. The place was intimidating…loud machines, forklifts running up and down the aisles carrying huge loads on pallets. There was a paging system that never seemed to stop and smoke from cutting metal filled the air as hot, metal chips fell into the bed of the huge machines. My job was to shovel those chips out and put them into heavy metal hoppers on wheels. It was a dirty and physically demanding job… an introduction to the real world. I grew up in a hurry!

The Axle was a three-shift/24 hour a day operation. Within those walls there was a job for everyone. In the shop and office there was a variety of jobs and if you bided your time you could get to one that suited you. The office was filled with employees doing everything manually in a time before computers. The shop floor was the same way. For the most part, in the machining areas there was one man per machine. There were also jobs in quality, stockroom, skilled trades, common labor, forklift, and others. Pay scales varied depending on the skill level that the job required. In 1963, most jobs were paying around $3.00 per hour. This was a huge amount of money. Overtime was being worked regularly, with employees given the opportunity to earn premium wages. Bringing home weekly paychecks between $100 and $200 a week was huge. People not employed there referred to it as the "Gold Coast".

The generation before me was a group of hard working people that earned their money. They were also extremely talented. The Axle had a variety of products, unlike that of the auto industry where people made or assembled the same thing day in and day out. Machinists had to know many different jobs because setting up and changing over a machine was complicated. The employees on these machines were good at this. Lacking formal job instructions, most of the skills to operate a machine came from memory and notes the operators made for themselves. They had to run their machine and manually setup for a new job, holding tolerances as close as .001 to .002 of an inch. To give an idea of how close a tolerance this is, a human hair has a thickness of about .007 of an inch. Many of these men were WWII veterans hired after the war. Others worked there through the war and were great role models and mentors to most of us.

The assembly line was another huge manufacturing area and it also required talent to assemble the many different models and products. The stockroom was huge and employees working there had to keep the assembly line and the machining areas stocked with the correct materials. Skilled trades, quality, and heat treat areas were all specialized and unique, crucial to keeping the operation going.

The onset of the computer age had the biggest impact to the manufacturing world. Manual machines were being replaced with computer-controlled machines. New technology meant one machine could now replace several manual machines. For the Axle it required a significant investment. With the new computerized machines costing an average of one million dollars apiece, it was cost prohibitive to replace all the machines at one time. The Axle was a combination of new and old. Many of the old workhorse machines were kept in service and you might see the million dollar machines next to a 1950s vintage machine. Machine cells were put together with one or two operators running several machines. The computer-controlled machines did not make the work easier for an operator. Machinists had to learn new skills to run these machines, edit programs, understand new types of tooling, and be careful not to cause damage to their expensive machine and tooling. It was the same in the office. The computer was also changing how the office created and stored information. I call this the third wave of the Industrial Revolution.

In the 1990s there was a new buzzword being used that caused workers to shudder. It was called outsourcing. I am not going to debate the pros and cons of this but at present the Axle, now AxleTech, has less than 100 people total, shop and office. The hundreds of machines are all gone and it is strictly an assembly plant. All manufactured parts are shipped into the plant from suppliers worldwide.

The Union

UAW Local 291 was organized in the late 1930s and represented the employees of the Axle in organized bargaining. The union still represents Axle employees today. My entire Axle career was working with the UAW, both as a member and then in management. The members of the union are very loyal and solidarity is strong. I worked with good union leaders and some that were more difficult. On the other hand, the Union dealt with management people, some reasonable and some not. Whatever the situation, both sides had to work together. Many times, people think that union and management have a "we" and "they" relationship. The Union has a very structured organization in the plant. There is a Union Committee that consists of a President, Vice President, Secretary, Treasurer, (2) Committee Men at large, and a Committee Man representing the skilled trades. Each shift has a Chief Steward and each department has a Departmental Steward. There is a contract that contains rules to operate the plant and explains the rights of the Company and the rights of those the Union represents. When the Company breaks the rules, the Union writes grievances. If the Union members break the rules, they are disciplined. Every week the Company and the Union would meet to try to resolve issues. If the issues could not be resolved, they would take the next step and eventually go to arbitration. This might sound like a very organized approach to resolve problems, but it is not. Very few of these issues go to arbitration. For the company, it can be expensive if you lose and many of the issues often sit in limbo. The best way to handle a problem when it comes up, is to work it out between the employee and the department Steward and the Supervisor. The Supervisor walks a fine line with his people. He has to worry about efficiency, scheduling the machines, controlling tooling costs, scrap, and maintaining a good relationship with those working for him. My first job in management was a first-line Supervisor and it was by far the toughest job I ever had.

Contract negotiations occur every 3 years. I was a member of the negotiating team for management during four negotiations. Sometimes negotiations would take months. I recall one negotiation in Cincinnati that lasted almost the entire summer. Contracts are usually written with a strike deadline date at the expiration of the agreement. Once that deadline draws near, negotiations will continue for hours as both sides work to try to resolve the remaining issues and avoid a work stoppage. No one really wants a strike. The Company loses credibility with their customers when shipments cannot be made, and the workforce loses wages that are seldom recovered by the increases from the new contract once settled. There are strategies in negotiations on both sides and the conversations across the table are generally civil. But occasionally when there are issues that neither side will budge on, negotiations are given a "time out" for each side to regroup and discuss the issue at hand. The Company knows that the contract has to be voted on by the membership for ratification. The timing of a tentative agreement is part of the strategy used sometimes by the Union. If settled too soon, the members may think the bargaining committee should have stayed at the table longer. Once the tentative agreement was reached, sometimes late at night or in the wee hours of the morning, someone at the Union Hall would take the call from the Union President, informing them to put the picket signs back in storage and instruct the employees to report to work at 7:00 a.m.

In my 43 years working there, I remember three strikes and one walkout, called a wildcat. All were short lived. The longest work stoppage lasted for a couple of weeks. During one work stoppage, it was decided that anyone within management, who could run a machine, was going to start machining and assembling parts. This is like asking anyone who has flown in a plane, to fly it. You know what it is supposed to do, but cannot figure how to make it work. Some management staff had been machinists at one time, and did well. Others drove forklifts and chipped out machines. Word leaked out to the Union that management was machining and producing axles. We did build some axles but could not ship them, as truckers would not generally cross a picket line. Through it all, we gained a new appreciation for what people did and how easy they made it look. We were glad to see the strike settled and went back to managing while the union members returned to their regular jobs.

If you were hired to work in the shop, it was a "closed shop" and everyone had to belong and pay dues to Local 291. Most of the people working there did not need to be disciplined, however, there were a few that received discipline and usually deserved it. Some of these people lost their jobs but those were the minority. Major discipline was given for drinking, stealing, running large amounts of scrap, and absenteeism.

Seniority is sacred in a union plant. In order to get a better shift or better job, you have to have seniority over anyone else who applies for it when posted. In a time of cutbacks, the junior people are laid off first. Layoffs are a disruption in the plant, but become a way of life for those affected. As long as there isn't a junior person in the plant doing what a senior person, who is laid off could do, everyone accepts that seniority prevails.

Management and the Union occasionally had issues and argued sometimes. But when there was a launch of a new product or there was a customer who moved up a delivery date, we all put the issues aside and made it happen. It was like a shot of adrenalin running through the plant. There was a huge pool of talent in Management and the Union and we all depended on each other to do their part. We also lived together outside the plant and there never was a distinction between shop and office when we met on the outside. Many friendships still exist and when retirees meet somewhere we talk about how lucky we were that the Axle was there for us.

The Diversions

People like to have fun at work. I call them diversions, but some call it horseplay and there are other words that are used also. I don't want to make it sound like this was a clown show. There are discreet things that go on, sometimes at the expense of others. Occasionally, they went beyond discreet and management had to step in. Much of what I am going to describe is probably no longer happening, but in 1963, the Axle was hiring many people and there was a combination of young and old. And it is fair to say the "old timers" occasionally liked to have fun at the expense of the "newbies". On third shift the diversions ran rampant. One of them was the painting of the shoes ritual. We marched in with our brand new safety shoes that had "new hire" written all over them. The Axle stenciled many of their parts, so there were cans of white spray paint at almost every machine. The game was to have an older employee engage you in conversation while another employee snuck up behind you and painted the heels of your shoes white. No one got mad and it was your badge of initiation into the 3rd shift.

Another diversion involved bluing. Bluing came in tubes about the size of toothpaste and about the same consistency. It was used for quality checks to see that parts were fitting together evenly. When a part was blued up and fitted to a mating part or a gauge, the bluing would indicate if there were high spots and show where they were. It was nasty stuff and it stained anything it came in contact with. If you got it on your hands you had to remove it with kerosene. Pranks included putting the bluing where someone would grab, like a lever on a machine, and get it on their hands. If you left your gloves out while you took a break, you might find the bluing in your gloves when you put them back on. I mentioned that sometimes these diversions got out of hand. One time they put bluing on one of the supervisors phones and then called him. That slowed things down for a long time. At some point the bluing and the painting of the shoes stopped and became only a memory of factory life from long ago.

There were other diversions in my early years. This was during a time when drinking was not frowned upon as deeply as it is today. Drinking was not only a diversion, but a problem with a few among the ranks. Some men, during their 20 minute lunch, jumped in their cars and hurried to a conveniently close tavern for a quick liquid lunch. It took 2 minutes to get there and 2 minutes back, so there was 16 minutes for beer and sometimes a shot of brandy. Hot ham and hot beef sandwiches were also served and the tavern knew who was coming and what they wanted. They would have everything set up and ready when the regulars would come in and have their drink or drinks and sandwich, then leave to get back to work before the buzzer, which didn't always happen. This was a ritual on all 3 shifts for the few that enjoyed a mid-shift beer and sandwich. This was slowed down when the company fenced in the parking lot, making the journey more time consuming. It stopped all together when UWO started buying property, which included the popular watering hole for the Axle.

Management monitored potential offenders and worked with the Union to attempt to resolve the issue of drinking during a work shift. When that failed, disciplinary action was imposed. Drinking was grounds for dismissal. This diversion was not unique to the Axle. It was fairly common for laborers in other companies to do the same things I described here.

Other diversions that went on were minor and management chose to look the other way. They were harmless things that cost little time, but if you put a stop to it you faced an angry work force. These are the same people you depend on every day. Things like football pools and check pools had the unwritten blessing of management. Radios were not allowed in the plant but if you wanted to have anyone work overtime on a Sunday when the Packers were playing, radio broadcasts of the game were overlooked. If you were a supervisor in the plant, you had your ear glued to one also.

Lawnmower and saw blades were sharpened by talented and skilled trades people, who were also adept at making things like sturgeon spears and ice chisels. Welding something for home was done in the weld booth. Management didn't stop this because they sometimes used the skills and expertise of these men to also do a favor for them. The expertise inside the walls of the Axle was phenomenal. There was nothing that could not be repaired, rebuilt, painted, or rewired. These diversions were commonly known internally as "government jobs".

CONCLUSION

The story of life at the Axle could be the same for others working in factories everywhere. The Axle, over the years, has been a large contributor to the local economy and the well-being of thousands of families in Oshkosh. They contributed thousands of dollars to charities. I have been in many other manufacturing facilities as part of my job over the years, and there are many similarities. But the biggest similarity is downsizing due to outsourcing and technology, allowing more work to be done with less people. Those of us who survived the downsizing have been fortunate. Many of those who lost their jobs and did not work to retirement, suffered great hardships when starting over. It is a way of life in manufacturing. You hire all you need during peak times for business, whether it is a boom in the economy or government spending to support a war. When these reasons for having increased levels of employment go away, the people are laid off and many never get to return. Sad but true. The Axle came close many times to moving out of the state or to another location in the city, or the property being sold to the University. Whatever happens in the future, it would be a terrible loss to ride down High Avenue and see the building at 1005 High Avenue not there. Whatever happens, those of us who spent much of our lives in those buildings are proud to have been a part of the business that, in our minds, will always be "THE AXLE"!

[1]Source: http://www.axletech.com/na_en/company/overview.php

ROBERT C. OSBORN

I t was a beautiful late autumn day. I was home working at my desk when the doorbell rang. Karen went to the door to find Phyllis Rothe, mother of my neighbor Tom Rothe, standing at the door smiling. "I found something Randy might enjoy" she said as she handed a large, red, hard cover book to Karen. She added, "I read Randy's book *Yesterday In Oshkosh* and just loved it! It brought back so many fond memories." The red book Mrs. Rothe had in her hand was titled *Osborn on Osborn* by Robert C. Osborn. "I've marked the pages where the author talks about Garlic Island. I know Randy is interested in the island and thought he might enjoy this," she said. Karen thanked Mrs. Rothe and said she would give the book to me.

Robert C. Osborn

Photo credit: Dick Benjamin.
Osborn on Osborn, Ticknor
and Fields

I sat the book aside, as I was working on several things at the time and promised myself I would get to it in time. I had not heard of Robert Osborn so my interest was diverted to other things I'd deemed more important.

A few times I picked up the book as I passed by my desk. I would randomly open to a page and start reading. I would put the book down, repeating the same routine from time-to-time. But the more I did this, the more interested I became in Robert Osborn.

It turns out the book was more than just some information on Garlic Island. Let me tell you about Robert Chelsey Osborn.

Robert Osborn was an artist whose drawings appeared in magazines such as the *New Yorker, Harper's* and *Vogue.* Some say Osborn was an artist, while others, including Osborn, considered his talents to be one of a "drawer". Cartoonist Garry Trudeau, best known for his cartoon strip *Doonesbury*, once wrote about Osborn, "…Robert Osborn is one of the very true masters of illustrated cartooning."

Robert C. Osborn was born in Oshkosh, Wisconsin on October 26, 1904, son of Albert Osborn and Alice Lydia Wyckoff. Albert was a self employed lumberman from Iola. He and his brother became lumbermen after purchasing an acre of timber in northern Wisconsin. That winter the two of them, aged seventeen and eighteen, lived in a canvas tent and cleared their entire one acre land of trees with a two-handled saw. They transported their lumber down the Mississippi River to St. Louis, where they sold the fruits of their labors. With the money they collected, the brothers returned to northern Wisconsin and purchased three more acres, sawed those trees, barged them south again, sold the logs, returned north once more and purchased another eight acres of timberland. This time the Osborn brothers hired woodsmen to do the work. Eventually, the brothers owned three lumber companies before moving to Oshkosh which was considered one of the largest lumber processing cities in the state. Also, it was believed the schools were better which was important when raising a family.

Robert's father and uncle had been quite successful in their lumber company ventures and relocated to Oshkosh with considerable wealth. Their sawmills in northern Wisconsin and Michigan were making so much money that in later years Albert told Robert "I didn't know how I would be able to spend it." Then came The Depression of 1929.

As I continued to read the life story of Robert Osborn, I was drawn into the warmth by his recollections of his early years growing up in Oshkosh.

Robert and his brother Chandler lived with their parents at 756 Algoma Street (now Algoma Blvd), a beautiful 32-room home with mechanically chipped stonework facing, high peaked roofs and chimneys, striped awnings, and Roman-esque arches. Considered by many as small-city affluence, the home featured a two-story living room with a barrel vault, a Tiffany lamp made of brass, and a Steinway concert grand piano. A root cellar, wine cellar, billiard room, hunting room and cook's quarters were also included. Out back a large and roomy barn had stalls large enough to hold two horses, a tack room, and ample room for a cow. Chickens were kept in a coop at the rear. An ice house would be filled each winter with large cakes of ice harvested from the frozen Fox River located only three blocks south of the Osborn home.

The house was located next door to the home of Stephan Radford, a well known Oshkosh lumberman in his own right. Robert recalled his neighbor Steven Radford. "…a totally impractical man. He started twenty-four different businesses; all of them failed. He used his wife's dowry until it had vanished." The Radford daughters Molly and Phyllis were near the same age as Robert and his brother Chandler.

As a child, Osborn enjoyed spending time with the Radford family on Garlic Island. He writes, "With Mrs. Radford's money, Mr. Radford bought an elm-covered island eight miles north of Oshkosh and a quarter of a mile from the mainland. On it were ten summer cottages, a caretaker's house, and a central dining hall." He continued, "We visited the two young daughters and the parents for a week each summer. There was a great deal of fishing, swimming, swinging in a frightening thirty-foot high rope swing, and walking around the island's perimeters." Osborn recalls learning how to swim at Garlic Island. "Mrs. Radford tied a line about my middle, fastened it to the end of a bamboo fishing pole, and walked up and down the big wooden dock set on its driven piles eight feet above me, calling down instructions as I slowly got the hang of it."

His boyhood memories on the island continued. "We would also 'think up' plays and produce them for the older people, who watched from the broad wooden porches that surrounded each cottage. Nearby, a large, white, mahogany-enclosed launch was used to transport local families out for the summer and bring the husbands out after work each afternoon. It tied up at the high, weathered dock overnight and departed for Oshkosh the next morning at seven-thirty. Mr. Radford's various schemes, such as planting sugar beets or importing Holland bulbs, to run the island at a profit gradually came to nothing and the place fell into decay."

Sunday afternoon drives to the country in the family's 1915 Packard were among Osborn's favorite memories. He describes the vehicle as "an enormous, lumbering four cylinder with two jump seats."

And as a teenage boy, the beauty of a woman was not wasted on young Robert Osborn. He was a bit smitten by the mother of his friend Seymour

Hollister. Osborn recalls his boyhood attraction to Mrs. Hollister. "Often after school, Seymour, black-bearded at thirteen, and I would walk the mile-and-a-half to his home, where we'd sprawl out on the thick, white rug in Mr. Hollister's study and listen in blinding ecstasy to George Gershwin's "Rhapsody In Blue" played by Paul Whiteman's band, time after 78- rpm-needle- bending time...At some point Mrs. Hollister would come down the white, ballustraded, scarlet –carpeted staircase, her peignoir flowing and noticeably parting. She would pass us, smile, lift up her lovely ivory ciga-rette holder and inhale, the cigarette tip glowing suddenly brighter-then she would turn from us and go out to talk to the cook."

Tragically, sometime later, Mrs. Hollister shortened her life by closing the garage doors behind their running Buick.

Enjoying the bounties the Oshkosh area offered, young Robert Osborn found enjoyment in sailing and duck hunting.

Sailboat racing, in scow-bottom, twenty-eight-foot boats was one of his favorites. One of a crew of five under skipper John Buckstaff, Osborn claims "Under the right 'reaching' conditions we once did one three-and–a-half-mile leg of a race at a speed of twenty-eight knots. He also built a forty-foot ice boat "carrying an enormous amount of sail" in which he claims to have traveled one hundred and twenty-two miles an hour on a straightway nine-mile run.

In 1908, Robert's father purchased an island on Lake Winnebago nine miles north of Fond du Lac. The island was named *The Fraction* and held seven duck blinds, allowing hunters to make corrections for the wind on any given day. Redhead, widgeon, pintail and greater and lesser scaup, aka bluebills, were plentiful. But for Osborn, the Canvas-back was his favorite, calling them "handsome, large, delicious to eat and almost as canny as any of the mallards and the few blacks we saw."

Robert attended High School in Oshkosh and then went to the University of Wisconsin-Madison in 1923. His parents paid the annual tuition of $16.50. A year later he applied and was transferred to Yale and went onto Paris, London and Rome to work and study abroad.

Robert took a great deal of pleasure in drawing. In his early years after college, Osborn gained fame getting his drawings published by *Harper's, Life, Look, Esquire, Time* and *Vogue* magazines. He had become famous for his publications in these national magazines, but not as famous as he would soon become. In late 1940, Osborn drew his first cartoon books, a series of three titled, *How to Shoot Ducks, How to Shoot Quail and How to Catch Trout.* That Christmas the series sold forty thousand copies and the royalty checks started rolling in. Osborn was getting a sense he finally found what he should be doing.

Photo Credit: Courtesy of Paul Giambarba, http://giam.typepad.com/100_years_of_illustration/osborn-robert-1904-1994/ and US Navy Air

On the morning of December 7, 1941, the Japanese attacked Pearl Harbor. The next day, Osborn enlisted in the US Navy. Assigned to the Navy Department in Washington DC, he decided to show his three shooting and fishing books to his commander A.K. Doyle. The officer had seen how the British Royal Air Force had produced training manuals using cartoons and assigned Osborn to a unit that produced *Sense Books.*

The US Navy *Sense Books* were a series of pamphlets with text and cartoons covering all manners of flying hazards. Dilbert was devised and characterized by Osborn as a dumb and cheerful cadet whose mistakes were a constant menace. His sketches showed pilots how ***not*** to fly and how to avoid accidents and death. Before he was through, Osborn drew some two thousand Dilbert posters about how not to fly, how to prepare and care for a plane, and how to avoid accidents and death. Osborn estimated he must have drawn over thirty thousand sketches, studies, printable drawings, and color overlays.

In addition to drawing training manuals, Osborn learned to fly and also served aboard a US Submarine. These experiences, he later related, helped him create effective training tools that were proven to save lives during combat. In fact, they deemed so effective that British RAF pilots found batches of Dilbert posters at the captured German airfields, reprinted in Germany and re-captioned in German.

While stationed in Washington, Osborn met the love of his life. Elodie Courter ran a department at the Washington Museum of art. She had a strong interest in the work being produced by Osborn's unit and stopped by one day to pay them a visit. It was love at first sight and the two were married shortly after Osborn arrived in Washington and right before he was sent to the Pacific.

His assignment brought him to the U.S.S. Essex where Osborn would see action in Saipan and Iwo Jima. Aboard the Essex was the pilot who taught Osborn to fly at the Atlanta Naval Station. During the battle for Saipan, the squadron in which he was assigned was attacked and his plane was hit. Osborn watched in horror as the pilot managed to be guided back some eighty miles to the Essex, blood streaming down his face, his sight failing, with two of his wing men giving him instructions. On board ship, it was obvious to Osborn and others that he was not going to make it down safely without crashing into the badly needed planes stationed on deck. With his fellow comrades watching, the pilot simply flew away into the dusk of the foreign sea. That image remained with Osborn all the days of his life; the view of a young man departing toward death's door.

Osborn returned to civilian life in 1945. He and wife Elodie had two sons; Nicolas and Eliot.

On December 20, 1994, Robert Chesley Osborn died at his home in Salisbury, Connecticut. His cause of death is listed as bone cancer. He was 90 years old.

"Finally, and perhaps most wonderful of all, are those things we tend to take for granted - the way genes behave, for one. I marvel endlessly at the correct placement of each tiny leg on even the most miniscule of insects; at the rhythmic order of life that has kept the mallard ducks we see today looking exactly like the ones that march by us in ancient Egyptian murals; in short, at the whole scheme of things, repeating or evolving under their own forces upon this earth."

-Robert Chesley Osborn (1904-1994)

Source: Osborn on Osborn by Robert C. Osborn; The Milwaukee Journal, January 16, 1983

GROWING UP IN THE 50S AND 60S

Life's learning's are achieved through the experiences we face on our journey from childhood through adulthood. Some better than others, but nonetheless important as they shape us in who we've become and what our children see in us...

-author unknown

Ah...the good old days.

That is what we call them you know. Everyone holds dear that special time in life while growing up...the formative years so they say. For me it was the 1950s and 60s.

The 1950s was a wonderful time in the life of a young boy. I'm certain it was for girls too, but in a totally different way.

I introduced you to my parents in my previous book, *Yesterday In Oshkosh...My Hometown.* Don and Geraldine (Ott) were my mom and dad. I grew up on the west side of town on Lark Street with my sister Debbie and brother Corey.

Born in1951, my earliest recollections begin when I was about four or five years old. It would be considered the "pre-kindergarten" years in a time where there was no pre-school, daycare, or other form of "early child development" centers allowing both parents to work. If both parents did work, the "caretaker" was called a baby sitter.

My mother did not work outside the home during those early years. She did, however, enjoy talking about working at the Diamond Match Company during the years before she was married. The Diamond Match Company was a large match manufacturing business located on High Street where the University of Wisconsin-Oshkosh campus resides today.

Later, mom also worked at Standard Kollsman assembling circuit boards. The company had recently relocated to Oshkosh in 1960 and was a manufacturer of television tuners and converters along with some aviation technology equipment. At its pinnacle, Standard Kollsman employed nearly 1200 workers in the Oshkosh location.

She also worked at Miles Kimball during the busy holiday season to earn a little extra money for Christmas. Miles Kimball was a catalogue company that specializes in selling personalized greeting cards, gifts, helpful household items, and unique products. The company continues in business today under the name Silver Star Brands.

My father worked more than one job during the early 50s. Mom and Dad married in January of 1950 and like most newlyweds didn't have much to start with. Dad drove a truck for Steffke Freight (later Spector Freight) during the day, then drove a taxi for Ollie Davies at Oshkosh's City Cab Company, and occasionally delivered pizzas for Jess and Nicks on nights and weekends. We would love it when occasionally a "prank" pizza order was called in and my dad would stop by the house unexpectedly with a pizza. If we were already in bed, my mom would wake my sister Debbie and me to enjoy the special treat with her.

I have some great memories of those younger years with my Dad. Like most boys in their pre-teens, your father was someone you admired and looked up to. I remember many of his favorite things and not surprisingly so, they soon became my favorites as well. He liked to season his food heavily with black pepper before even tasting it…so do I. He was best at cooking BBQ chicken on the grill…so am I. In the 50s, dad had a charcoal grill that rested on three legs and featured an aluminum hood and cover which spanned about half the cooking surface. A small rotisserie motor was attached to the side of the hood where you would insert a long metal rod with clamps that would neatly hold two whole chickens and turn ever so slowly over the hot bed of coals. BBQ sauce would be added about halfway through the cooking cycle. The sauce and juices would drip onto the coals and give off the most wonderful aroma you could ever imagine. When done, you had the best, most delicious, crispy BBQ'd chicken ever! My technique today differs a bit from dads' as I use a kettle type grill, cook indirect and add apple wood chips for a little extra smoky flavor. It may not be the same, but I think nonetheless he would be proud to know I'm carrying on his tradition. My youngest daughter, Brooke, always calls it "Dad's World Famous BBQ Chicken."

As most boys will do, there came a time when my confidence grew to a point where I was ready to challenge my dad. One evening, after supper, dad was sitting at the kitchen table enjoying his after dinner cigarette. He asked me to do something and I more or less shrugged it off. He said he would get up and whoop my butt if I didn't do it. I told him, "You'll have to catch me first". Well let me tell you…I really underestimated what that 'old man' (about age 30) could do. He was out of his chair like a shot as I blew through the back screen door of the house and headed across the yard. I thought I was gaining a lead on him when he suddenly hurdled a three-foot cedar tree like a gold medal Olympian and grabbed me by the collar of my shirt. We fell to the ground both laughing so hard I think I was in tears. Needless to say, I never talked back to my dad again.

As a young boy, the attire for the day depended on what was going on. On non-school days, it was usually blue jeans or "overalls" as they were called then. They were durable and perfect for playing outside. As boys would do, we gave them a real workout climbing trees and crawling on dirt piles. They were usually cuffed at the bottom as Mom said I grew too fast and always bought them at least one size bigger than I needed…thus the cuff. "You'll grow into 'em," she would say when I complained they were too big. Girls were not into jeans so much. "Clam Diggers" were the style and that fashion seemed to come and go through the years. To best describe them they were long shorts that went between the knee and ankle. Then the style changed to "Pedal Pushers" which were not much different than "Clam Diggers" other than slightly shorter but still knee length. The name "Pedal Pushers" was derived as active wear that allowed girls to ride bikes more comfortably. Today, the style is still fashionable and known as "Capri's" (back to below knee length).

As I grew into adolescence, I became more conscious of my appearance as I started to notice that girls were more than just an annoyance. Suddenly, personal grooming became important.

As most boys did, we combed our hair back, usually with a part on one side, and used some of the fine products for men that were designed to give your look more appeal. Hair care products were a 'must have' to look your best. *Vitalis with V7*® was promoted as a "greaseless grooming discovery" while *Wildroot Cream Oil*®, the hair tonic with lanolin, kept dryness out and grooming in. Me? I was a *Brylcream*® guy. As the ad jingle explained, "Brylcream…a little dab'l do ya…Brylcream… you'll look so debonair…Brylcream…the gals'l all pursue ya…they'll love to get their fingers in your hair." Then came the finishing touch. Splash on a little cologne, usually *British Sterling®* or *Jade East®*, (which we purchased downtown at The Golden Hanger or The Canterbury Shop), and I was good to go! By the mid 1960s, the wet head was dead and the new dry look was in.

The 50s was also a time when the world continued healing from the effects of WWII. We saw the tensions of the 'Cold War' between the US and the Soviet Union escalate as social differences between Capitalism and Communism came to the forefront, first with the Korean War (1950-1953) followed by Castro's Cuban Revolution in 1959. The testing of nuclear weapons by the US and Russia hinted of the possibility of nuclear war. Air raid sirens were installed nationwide as part of our nation's Civil Defense System. Today those same sirens are used for severe weather alerts.

In 1950, a new term emerged, further fueling the tensions around the Cold War…"McCarthyism". Senator Joe McCarthy from Wisconsin began making public claims that groups of communists and communist sympathizers were among us, fueling widespread paranoia and false accusations.

In Southeast Asia, tensions were rising in Vietnam, Laos and Cambodia. In what would become known in the US as one of the most contentious wars in our country's history, North Viet Nam, backed by Russia, China and other pro communist countries, began their campaign to unite all of Viet Nam as one country under communist rule. The US saw this move as a potential spread of communism as if one state went communist, others would follow. The US involvement in the Viet Nam war quietly began in the early 1950s when advisors were dispatched to French Indochina and ended with the fall of Saigon on April 30, 1975. The price to America was devastating. Dealt with heavy losses, over 58,000 American soldiers were killed or missing and over 300,000 wounded. Draft Lotteries were held to fill the need for "boots on the ground" in Southeast Asia. In 1970, the draft for men who turned 19 years of age that year put me right near the top at number 004. I had already enlisted in the Wisconsin National Guard in 1968 and ending up serving a 20+ year enlistment in the 1157 Transportation Company, of which I am very proud.

The turbulent times escalated and carried into the 60s. Cold War tensions were elevated by several key events including the failed invasion of Cuba to overthrow dictator Fidel Castro and the Russian attempt to build arms in Cuba became what was known as the Cuban Missile crisis. President Kennedy and Soviet Premier Nikita Khrushchev played a dangerous chess game that took the world to the brink of nuclear war.

The assassinations of political and civil rights leaders left a gaping hole in the hearts of Americans who wondered where our country was heading. On November 22, 1963 President John F. Kennedy was assassinated in a motorcade in Dallas. His brother Robert F. Kennedy was killed in the kitchen of a hotel following his speech claiming victory in the California primary for President of the United States in 1968. Also in 1968 in Memphis, civil rights leader Dr. Martin Luther King was shot and killed while standing on his hotel balcony. And in 1965, former Islam Nation leader Malcolm X was gunned down in a Manhattan ballroom.

Russia started what would become known as the "Space Race" when they launched *Sputnik,* an unmanned satellite into orbit on October 4, 1957. A month later, they followed up by launching a dog named *Laika* into orbit. In January of 1958, the US launched Explorer 1, the first US satellite to reach orbit. This back and forth continued until April of 1961 when Russian Yuri Gagerin became the first man in space. One month later, Alan Shepard became the first American to break the bonds of earth and just three short weeks later, our country's new President, John F. Kennedy addressed Congress challenging the nation to put a man on the moon by the end of the decade.

The space race continued throughout the 1960s with Russia and the US racing to put the first man on the moon. In July of 1969, American Neil Armstrong became the first human to set foot on the lunar surface.

The 50s also saw Alaska and Hawaii added as the 49th and 50th state in 1959 while Presidents Harry S. Truman and Dwight D. Eisenhower led our country through some very difficult and turbulent times.

Television, which emerged in the 1940s, was quickly growing in popularity and by the end of the fifties most homes had one.

Evening TV programs were probably the most common form of entertainment we enjoyed as a family. Dad liked gangster movies, especially if it featured Edward G. Robinson or Robert Stack as Elliott Ness on the *Untouchables*. Mom preferred westerns, and of course, romance movies. Her favorite actor was Victor Mature who she would swoon over every time he appeared on television. My dad would huff and say something like, "What's so special about him?"

The Dead End Kids (also known as The Bowery Boys) were usually on Sunday mornings. It was one of the few times during the week that dad was home and not working. He would laugh out loud at Leo Gorcey as "Slip" Mahoney and Huntz Hall as "Sach" Jones portrayed their characters as "street kids" in New York City.

The *Sunday Funnies* was broadcasted weekly on WTMJ, Channel 4 in Milwaukee. In good weather, we would adjust the antennae on our roof with the rotor located on top of our TV set from its normal position of northeast toward Green Bay, to the south and Milwaukee...how convenient! The program showed several of the comic strips from the Sunday edition of the *Milwaukee Journal* with someone reading them to you as the camera panned the strip in close-up fashion.

1950s television programming was an entertainment explosion. Despite only three network channels to view (ABC, CBS and NBC), we never felt shortchanged on entertainment. Oshkosh even had its own television station with WOSH-TV. Its life was short lived however, lasting less than a year from 1953-1954, so it was gone before I was old enough to watch TV. So many wonderful old programs became classics that are still watched today on cable, satellite, and the internet.

Lucille Ball and Desi Arnez held the number one spot in the 50s for years with *I Love Lucy*. *The Adventures of Ozzie and Harriet* depicted daily life in "suburbia" through the Nelson family and introduced us to a young rock star-to-be, Ricky Nelson. *Leave It To Beaver* had us believe that each day Mom wore a nice dress, high heels, pearl necklace, and earrings while doing housework and looking after "The Beav". Hitchcock scared the daylights out of us with *Alfred Hitchcock Presents* and Rod Serling made it difficult to sleep at night with tales from *The Twilight Zone*. Jackie Gleason, Audrey Meadows and Art Carney were *The Honeymooners* and we laughed at Red Skelton laughing at himself.

Westerns were big in the 50s, In fact, the top ten television programs in 1958 were westerns. *Gunsmoke, Wagon Train, Have Gun Will Travel, The Rifleman, Maverick, Tales of Wells Fargo,* and *The Life and Legend of Wyatt Earp* made the top ten while others like *Sugarfoot, Rawhide* (who introduced us to Clint Eastwood as a young Rowdy

Yates), *The Adventures of Rin Tin Tin, Annie Oakley, Broken Arrow, The Adventures of Wild Bill Hickok, The Lone Ranger,* and too many others to mention, gave us hours of viewing pleasure. The King of the Cowboys, Roy Rogers with wife Dale Evans, Trigger the Golden Palomino, and Bullet the Wonder Dog left us feeling good as they rode off into the sunset singing "Happy Trails".

"Out of the clear blue of the western sky comes Sky King!" A modern day western of sort, Sky King, along with niece Penny and her brother Clipper flew their Cessna T-50 "Songbird" on an adventure every week capturing bad guys and finding lost souls from their Flying Crown Ranch in Arizona.

Most of us "Baby Boomers" grew up with black and white televisions. Although colored TV was invented in the early 50s, it wasn't until the end of that decade that color programming was readily available. My cousins were the first people we knew to own a color TV. We would go to their house to watch programs like *Bonanza* and *Walt Disney's Wonderful World of Color*. The NBC peacock would fill the screen with his tail fanned open showing bright, vibrant colors while the network announcer informed us, "Brought to you in living color on NBC".

Sunday morning TV was pretty much relegated to the local stations as the only network programming offered a few news programs like *Meet The Press*. The local Green Bay TV stations featured a number of polka bands every Sunday morning. Romy Gosz was the 'King of Polkas' by his own modest self admission. Gosz also claimed to be "the world's only dance band blessed by Pope Pius XII." Alvin Styczynski, the Polish Prince from Pulaski, Wisconsin, had a polka program on WBAY-TV for nine years. *The Dick Rodgers Show* debuted in 1955 and held that spot on WLUK-TV for 23 years. John Check and the Wisconsin Dutchmen debuted in 1967, also on WLUK-TV. Check, who had a PhD in Educational Psychology, headed the Educational Psychology Department at Wisconsin State College in Oshkosh in 1966. Dr. Check spoke with a heavy Polish accent, and I remember him shopping at the Super Valu grocery store where I worked on Sawyer Street. *The Polka Festival Show* debuted in 1967 and aired on Saturday nights from 9:30-10pm. After two months, the program was expanded to one hour and even topped the *CBS Saturday Night Movie* in ratings that year.

For music, the 50s was a wonderful time with artists like Frank Sinatra, Bing Crosby, Nat King Cole, and Tony Bennett ushering in the "Crooner" era. It was also the birth of rock 'n roll. Legendary greats like Chuck Berry, Jerry Lee Lewis, The Everly Brothers, and Buddy Holly introduced us to something that would change the music scene forever. The "Doo Wop" groups like The Platters, The Drifters, and The Coasters gave us that velvety smooth sound while "Rockabilly" was popularized by artists like Elvis and Bill Haley.

One of my favorite memories was listening to the tunes coming out of the old Seeburg jukebox at the Fox River Bar on Wisconsin Ave. It was where my dad liked to stop for a couple of beers on occasion and sometimes he would let me tag along. I'd beg him for a quarter and plug it into that beautiful music machine. You could hear the coin as it slid down the slot, making the jukebox light up and come to life. It held vinyl 45 rpm records and for twenty-five cents I was allowed six selections. My favorites were easy choices and I most always played the same songs. The honky tonk sound of Johnny Cash and his trademark "guitar plunk" as he growled out "Walk The Line" and "What Do I Care?", Ray Price's "For The Good Times", and Sheb Wooley's "Purple People Eater". On occasion I would ask Ness, the bartender, to "turn it up" for me, as he could control the volume with a dial behind the bar.

These new sounds drew young fans into the world of music. Some of which were very difficult to accept by the "older generation" who would complain and criticize lyrics like …"Who put the bomp in the bomp-bah-bomp-bah-bomp? Who put the ram in the ramma lamma ding dong?"... (a big hit for The Viscounts in 1961). Elvis' hip gyrations were too much for network censors as they blacked out his lower half while performing on the Ed Sullivan Show in 1957. Elvis was known as "The King" and loved by millions of adoring fans. Men changed their hairstyles and grew sideburns. Girls swooned every time his songs came on the radio. My mother loved Elvis and his music so much that she named her miniature poodle Lisa Marie after Elvis' daughter.

The birth of rock 'n roll in the 1950s also laid the groundwork for a group of four mop-haired, teenaged musicians from Liverpool, England. The Beatles took America by storm in 1964 and the music scene would never be the same again. Many of our favorite artists that established deep roots in the 50s found themselves quickly fading into obscurity. New groups like The Rolling Stones, The Dave Clark Five, Herman's

Hermits, The Beach Boys, and others took over record sales almost overnight.

The release of albums such as The Beatles *Sgt. Pepper's Lonely Hearts Club Band* and Brian Wilson's *Pet Sounds* took rock music to a whole new level. For me, it was the beginning of the "Psychedelic Era" when artists like Jim Morrison and The Doors released "Light My Fire", Jimi Hendricks gave us "Purple Haze", Janis Joplin screeched out "Me and Bobby McGee", and Creams' Jack Bruce, Ginger Baker, and Eric Clapton wrote hits like "Sunshine of Your Love" and "Tales of Brave Ulysses".

In 1967, I remember stopping into a small store on Ohio Street that sold incense, beads, tie dyed shirts, posters, and other kinds of "groovy" things. I purchased a psychedelic poster of the Beatles and a "black light" that looked "really keen" hanging on my bedroom wall. I would play the Beatles' *Magical Mystery Tour* album over and over again while my lava lamp slowly gyrated to the sounds of the 60s.

Each week, my buddy Garrett Galica and I would spend hours, and our weekly paychecks from Stangel's, at the Exclusive Company located on Main Street in downtown Oshkosh. We were on a first name basis with owner Mr. Giambetti and store manager, Mr. Martin. The Exclusive Company was stocked with thousands of 45 rpm records, including all the latest hits. 45s sold for 99 cents each. The long aisle that reached from the front door to the back of the store was filled with racks of albums or LP's (33 1/3 rpms). Albums sold for $4.99 for stereophonic and $3.99 for monaural. During that time when I was a teen, I accumulated quite a record collection which I still own (and play) today.

Radio stations had disc jockeys to play records and entertain us with their personalities. "Wolfman" Jack gained national fame in the 60s with his raspy voice and wolf howl as he spinned the hits. Casey Kasem debuted in 1970 and featured his American Top 40 list. From 1958-1967 New York DJ Murray the K filled the airwaves and is credited with discovering great talents like Bobby Darin and Dionne Warwick.

But the all time king of TV music personalities was Dick Clark. *American Bandstand* debuted on ABC in 1957 with Clark as the host. He spent the next 30 years introducing us to new music and entertainers. The program, filmed in a studio in Philadelphia, featured regular kids dancing to the hits as Clark introduced them.

By the end of the decade, rock music left its landmark footprint at Woodstock in a music festival attended by over 400,000 people on a 600 acre farm in New York State. Rock 'N Roll was here to stay!

Because of the large eastern European influence by immigrants that settled in this area, there were many polka bands around Oshkosh in the 50s and 60s. Local bands featured John Check and the Wisconsin Dutchmen, Dodo Ratchman, Sam Ostwald, Bill Novotny, Ralph Becker and the Harmonettes, just to name a few. Dodo Ratchman worked days at Rockwell (Wisconsin Axle) and led his band for over 50 years. In his youth, Ratchman signed a professional contract with the St. Louis Cardinals baseball team. Every wedding reception featured a polka band, it was a Wisconsin tradition. Guests would "E-I-E-I-E-I-O" the night away and nobody liked a good "Flying Dutchman" more than us hearty Wisconsin folk.

Have you ever thought back about things you did or had in the 50s and 60s that somehow became lost or faded with the evolution of time?

Taverns were forced to close on Election Day and grocery stores and businesses locked their doors on all major holidays like Easter, Christmas, and Thanksgiving Day. On Good Friday, businesses closed from noon until 3pm so employees had the chance to attend church.

Carbonated soft drinks like Coke® and Pepsi® came in glass bottles available mostly in 12oz and 16oz sizes. The 12oz size came in 6-pack cartons while the 16oz size was usually sold in 8-pack cartons. Here in Oshkosh it was always referred to as "pop", never soda. If you couldn't finish your "pop", we had little stainless steel stoppers with rubber closures that operated with a plunger. It would keep your pop carbonated for a few extra days. There were no plastic 2-liter bottles. Quart size glass bottles of Penguin mixes were popular during the holiday season. Club Soda and Sour mix was used to make highballs and could be purchased in most supermarkets or at the Harra Beverage Mart. Harra's, located on Ceape Ave, carried regional brands like Harra®, Jic Jac® and Goody®. We loved to go to Harra's with our dad to get a case of pop. The Goody brand offered many different flavors and Harra's would let you mix and match the case with the flavors you liked best. Root Beer, Lemon-Lime, Cream Soda, Grape, Black Cherry,

Orange were our favorites. Twenty four - 10oz bottles came neatly packed in a wooden case with the Harra Beverage name painted proudly on the side.

Remember *Fizzies®*? Drop one of these fruit flavored tablets into a glass of water and watch it fizz! In 1968, the FDA banned certain food additives and artificial sweeteners like cyclamates. Cyclamates were an essential ingredient in making *Fizzies* and scientists then didn't know how to reformulate the recipe and *Fizzies* soon disappeared from grocery shelves. (Note: *Fizzies* are back today with new formulas and expanded flavors from the original five.)

Looking Back...

Kurtz Pony Rides at Menominee Park, 1956
Photo Credit: Deb Bradley

And who can forget *Fizz-Niks®*! Modeled after the Russian Spaceship Sputnik, the *Fizz-Nik* turned an ordinary bottle of pop into an ice cream soda. The device was a plastic sphere that separated in half and had an open spout on each end. You inserted one half into the bottle of your favorite soda, add a scoop or two of vanilla ice cream, then snap the other half on and drink. I remember after one drink and the ice cream started to melt, it would run back down into the bottle. Needless to say the concoction was not very inviting and we lost interest in *Fizz-Niks* rather quickly.

Coffee was brewed in an electric percolator. A lovely chrome finished stainless steel pot with a long, slender pouring spout, plastic handle, and a small glass bubble dome on top that allowed you to watch the coffee brew. The pot was first filled with water. You then put coffee grounds into a small metal basket that had a lid with small holes on the top. A long metal stem would then be inserted into the bottom of the basket, and then the stem/basket assembly was placed inside the pot. As the water percolated it would travel up the stem, into the glass bulb on top, and drip into the basket of coffee grounds, eventually turning the water into rich black coffee.

Food in the 50s and 60s was interesting to say the least. Farmers would come into town with their pickup trucks loaded with fresh produce and drive slowly through the neighborhoods. Potatoes, tomatoes, melons, cukes, apples, squash, cabbages, green beans, sweet corn...you name it. All raised locally and as fresh as can be. Prior to the early 50s, mom and pop grocery stores had little or no refrigeration. If you wanted fresh produce, you could drive into the country and visit one of the numerous farms stands or wait until the farm trucks came to your neighborhood. The Bradley egg farm was located just a few miles west of Oshkosh and we would visit there regularly to get farm fresh eggs.

Our family was of german heritage so many of my mother's recipes were handed down through several generations of kraut eaters. She made the best head cheese at Christmas time. Those of us who grew up eating it couldn't wait for her to make it, as it was pretty much an annual event. Those that weren't raised in the german family tradition would ask, "How can you eat that stuff?" Originally, head cheese was made by boiling the meat off the head of a hog. Times were difficult and you needed to make use of every part of the animal. In my meat cutting days, we would joke that every part of the animal was used except the squeal...and now they record that! Today, because fresh hog's heads are hard to find...we use pork hocks. To uphold the family tradition, I still make mom's head cheese recipe every Christmas.

Another culinary delight that fits into this same category is "cracklins", also sometimes known as "scraps". Cracklins are pieces of pork skin and fat left over from the lard rendering process. Pieces of cooked scraps were cut into small pieces and salted. Some pieces you would chew for 10 minutes and then have to spit out because it was never going to break down. I'm afraid if we had nutritional labeling back then, imagine what deep fried pork fat with salt would look like!

My mom was a great cook, as most moms were in those days. Eating out was a big treat, not part of the daily eating ritual it is today. She made a dish she called "kahoctus". Not sure where the name came from, but it was good. Simply put, it was hamburger, onions and finely diced potatoes mixed together. When served, we would pour pancake syrup over the top. Her homemade chili was the best, using mostly fresh ingredients…tomatoes, onions, celery, green peppers, and lean ground beef. Add a can of kidney beans, a healthy dash of chili powder, a couple of bay leaves, and some elbow macaroni…chili made Wisconsin style!

One of our family's favorite meals was baked chicken. Mom would go to the Schubert Meat Market on Oshkosh Avenue, and buy a fresh, whole chicken and bring it home wrapped neatly in crisp white butcher's paper. Once she removed the chicken from its wrap, she would take the chicken over to the gas stove and turn on one of the front burners. Holding the chicken by its feet, she would methodically turn it slowly over the flames to burn off the hair. Then she would painstakingly remove any pin feathers that were still attached. The bird was now ready for cooking.

Cigarettes were only 25¢ per pack. They were sold in grocery stores on racks right at each checkout lane. Places like bars, restaurants, and bowling alleys would have cigarette vending machines that usually carried the top 8-10 brands. *Winston®, Marlboro®, Camel®, Chesterfield®, Viceroy®,* and *Lucky Strike®* were among the top selling brands. Ashtrays were a common fixture in almost every home as most people smoked. Some ashtrays were simple designs and sat on coffee tables and end tables, while others were more elaborate and came on a stand like a furniture accessory. For men, smoking was considered masculine and for the ladies it was glamorous. You could smoke virtually anywhere and everywhere. There were few restrictions. I used to find it humorous that airplanes had smoking and non-smoking sections as everyone was exposed to the same long tube of unventilated air.

Easter was a special time for kids back then just as it is today. I remember going into the Sears Roebuck store located on Merritt

Avenue, one block east of Main Street in downtown Oshkosh. In the center aisle of the store that led from the main entrance, was a large table, with a clear plastic edge surrounding all four sides, filled with live baby chicks. The chicks were dyed different colors - pink, purple, green. Above the table were several heat lamps to keep the chicks warm. If you think the cereal aisle at the grocery store is a challenge to navigate kids through, imagine this. It was also not uncommon to get a live baby bunny at Easter. My sister and I had a bunny that we trained to go to the bathroom on newspaper we spread on the basement floor. When the bunny became a rabbit, he was taken out to the country where my dad's friend owned a farm, and I'm sure he lived a long happy life. At least that's what we were told.

Cap guns were in every boy's toy collection. A roll of paper caps were inserted into the gun and when the trigger was pulled, the hammer drew back and forth igniting the tiny amount of gunpowder, imitating the sound of a gun being shot. Today, displaying that same toy would ignite a response from the police tactical squad… but that, I guess, is the sign of the times in which we now live.

When it rained or snowed, galoshes were a necessity for every kid to keep his shoes from being ruined. They fit right over your shoes and had five adjustable buckles which allowed you to tuck in your pant legs and snug the boot up tight.

It was always fun when road construction came into the neighborhood. A fresh layer of stone would be laid down. We would spend hours scouring through the freshly laid rock looking for "fools gold." Those "priceless" nuggets would glisten in the sun and we would imagine we had just accumulated a fortune. Traffic barricades would be put in place with a smudge pot or two to warn cars of impending danger. Smudge pots were black metal ball-shaped containers filled with kerosene. A wick protruded from the top and when lit would burn for days.

Sometime in the late 1950s, it was decided that I needed to have my tonsils removed. As I recall, it seemed rather common to do this, particularly if one was experiencing sore throats. It required an overnight stay at Mercy Hospital and I remember during recovery eating alot of *Jell-O*™ and ice cream to help soothe the pain. When we went home, the tonsils went with us. They were put in a small jar with a tightly fitted glass lid and preserved in a somewhat clear liquid I assume was formaldehyde. That jar, with my two tonsils floating inside, sat on my mother's bedroom dresser for several years. Occasionally, my curiosity would draw me in for a visit. I'd spin the jar a little, never giving a second thought on why we would want to do this. One day they were gone.

Laundry detergents were strictly powdered and always came packed in a large cardboard carton. Products like *Tide®* and *Oxydol®* were the brands my mother preferred. Other companies, like *Duz®*, would include free merchandise to entice customers into using their product. Glassware was included inside each carton. *Breeze®* detergent offered free bath or kitchen towels in their larger box and washcloths and dishcloths in the smaller cartons.

Like most boys my age in the 50s, I was always looking for things to do to earn some money. Unlike today, the revenue stream coming from mom and dad back then was minimal. If you wanted to buy a pack of baseball cards, a pop from the vending machine, or maybe one of those delicious *Alaska Pops®*, you needed to find a way to earn some extra money. In the winter, we would go door to door in our neighborhood offering to shovel snow, or during the summer months, cut grass. Our lawnmower was one without an engine. It was a reel type mower that you pushed. And you didn't want to wait too long between cuttings as the grass became too high, it was more difficult to mow.

Now, as I look back on those days of my youth, I realize many of the things I have taken for granted. We didn't have a bunch of expensive toys and gadgets, but spent hours and hours making our own fun. We played outside in the summer months until the streetlights came on. We would ride our bikes all over town and not worry about a thing. Our bikes didn't have locks. We didn't need them. At home we didn't lock the front and back door every night like we do today. We respected our elders and people of authority. We addressed adults as Mr. or Mrs. Talking back or being disrespectful to a teacher or policeman was simply unheard of...unless you were a juvenile delinquent.

And families did more visiting back then. Our aunts, uncles, and cousins would drop in, sometimes several times a week. The adults would sit in the kitchen, smoking and drinking coffee while the kids played games in the bedroom, the basement, or weather permitting, outside.

I believe that was a carryover from the days before there was television. If you look at many of the homes built prior to 1950, most had large front porches. Folks would sit out on the porch and visit with passerby's and neighbors. In the summer there was no indoor air conditioning other than a fan or two, so the porch was a good place to cool off with an evening breeze.

Ah…the good old days. That's what we call them you know.

Source: (1)Oshkosh, 100 Years a City, Clinton F. Karsteadt, Editor;

EPILOGUE

Preserving local history is important. I'd like to think in some small way writing this book, and the one previous, is my contribution to the responsibility we all share. Each time we lose another old home or building, we lose a piece of our past.

A look around our community shows we are proud of our city's heritage. The beautiful and historical Grand Opera House and the Legion on the Lake (now known as The Waters) have returned to their full glory as places for special events. The Edgar Sawyer residence is now our Public Museum and the home of one of Oshkosh's most successful lumber barons is the stately Paine Art Center. The home of John Rodgers Morgan (Morgan Lumber Company) is a beautifully restored Victorian house, furnished the way it may have looked in 1888. Everywhere we look in Oshkosh, we can't help but marvel at the architectural designs of William Waters. All of these projects required a huge amount of resources including time, people and money.

We, as a community can make a difference by finding a workable solution to create a functional use for these historic treasures. Not everything can or should be turned into a museum. For years, professional people have run their businesses from some of the old homes on Algoma Boulevard, and have not disturbed the original look and design of the house. We can support the business owners located on historic Main Street by shopping locally. We can get involved with groups like the Oshkosh Landmarks Commission, The Oshkosh Public Museum, or the Winnebago County Historical and Archaeological Society and work to create more historic designation around the neighborhoods of our fine city. Tax breaks through historic designations can be incentives for people who want to own a home in a historic district.

Consider donating your time by volunteering at The Oshkosh Public Museum, The Grand Opera House, The Winnebago County Historical and Archaeological Society, or the Paine.

Oshkosh is a city with a long, rich history. Let's take pride in our local history. Let's stand up and work to preserve it for future generations.

ACKNOWLEDGEMENTS

As an author, one of the things I quickly learned is that writing a book requires the assistance and support of many people. It is here I wish to thank those to whom I am indebted, as it is through their work, input, opinions and willingness to share their life's experiences that has allowed me to make this journey possible.

Karen Domer
Heather Domer Connors
Theda Eckstein
Abe Eckstein
Ben Joas
Pete Christiansen
Jim Senderhauf
David Metzig
Phyllis Rothe
Kelly Zdanovec
Dan Radig
Ed Tiedje
Jim Backus
Dylan Postl
Bob Hergert
Ralph Hergert
Ron Hergert
Warren Hergert
Mark Spanbauer

Mary Schulz Kruger
Steven Juedes
Vern Gauger
Jeffery Steinert
Charlotte Schulz Christen
Jim VandeHei
John and Joan VandeHei
Ethel Green
Deb Daubert
Scott Cross
Judy Nitkowski Engleman
Clarence Jungwirth
John Dorcey
Peter Moll
Mara Munroe
Patrick Flanigan
Ken Kohlwey
Vivian Hazell

A special thanks to my wife **Karen** and daughter **Heather** for their invaluable assistance with editing and proofing.

For more Oshkosh history and wonderful memories, pick up your copy of:

YESTERDAY IN OSHKOSH ...MY HOMETOWN

RANDY R. DOMER